What's in a Phrase?

What's in a Phrase?

Pausing Where Scripture Gives You Pause

Marilyn Chandler McEntyre

William B. Eerdmans Publishing Company
Grand Rapids, Michigan / Cambridge, U.K.

Published 2014 by Wm. B. Eerdmans Publishing Co.
2140 Oak Industrial Drive n.e., Grand Rapids, Michigan 49505 /
P.O. Box 163, Cambridge cb3 9pu U.K.
www.eerdmans.com

Printed in the United States of America

20 19 18 17 16 15 14   7 6 5 4 3 2 1

Library of Congress Cataloging-in-Publication Data

isbn 978-0-8028-7114-5

Contents

Contents

Invitation and Admonition

Contents

Mystery and Surprise

Introduction

P HRASES HAVE LIVES OF THEIR OWN. Neither sentences nor single words, they are little compositions that suggest and evoke and invite. They don't, like the sentence, declare or ask or command. They are often what we remember: "Fourscore and seven years ago" recalls a whole era, triggers a constellation of feelings, and evokes an image of Lincoln. "Inherit the earth" carries the weight of promise, the rhythm of the Beatitudes, and a vision of Jesus on a hillside. We can hardly hear "a mighty fortress" without recalling the invigorating strains of the hymn and its dignified parade of images. In the classic film *A Bridge Too Far*, one soldier, rowing for his life away from an impending explosion, repeats again and again a fragment of the only prayer he remembers: "Hail Mary, full of grace. . . . Hail Mary, full of grace. . . . Hail Mary, full of grace . . ." — and somehow we believe that such a prayer at such a time suffices. I have known people far into old age and dementia who can be awakened with a little shock of recognition by a familiar phrase; one aged English teacher applauded when she heard a line from Keats's "The Eve of St. Agnes," and one of her neighbors, largely incoherent, recited the entire 100th Psalm when she heard a reader begin, "Make a joyful noise . . ."

Phrases are powerful instruments of awakening and recollection for all of us. The wisdom of the ancient Benedictine practice of *lectio divina* or "holy reading" lies in focusing not on an idea or even a sentence, but on a "word or phrase" that summons us to attention. Learning to notice what we notice as we move slowly from words to meaning, pausing where we sense a slight beckoning, allowing associations to emerge around the phrase that stopped us is an act of faith that the Spirit will meet us there. There is, we may assume, a gift to be received wherever we are stopped and summoned. At one reading of the prologue to John's Gospel, it may be that "In the beginning" allows us a moment to step outside time and revel in a cosmic awe that brings with it the comfort that we are not stuck in the morass of human history, but belong to a much bigger story. At another reading of the same passage, it may be the simple phrase "with God" that gives us occasion to consider the mystery of divine companionship that is an aspect of God's very being.

The reflections in this book are my small acts of obedience to such summonings. They are informed by the spirit of *lectio divina*, though they do not reflect the strictly prescribed devotional practice. I chose biblical phrases that have been stopping points for me, hoping that sharing what those phrases opened up might be of value to readers. I hope they will encourage you to find your favorite phrases and try the same exercise of sitting with them and seeing what they bring up. The writing of this book has served purposes for me beyond what I anticipated; I hope these meditations serve your purposes also, and that they may encourage you to see words within the Word as invitations, summoning you as you read to go *in* for a little while before you go *on,* and in doing so to find that the little phrases are places of divine encounter, epiphany, or unexpected guidance. I offer them with the prayer that they may add a few threads to the rich weave of conversation among people who share a belief that the living Word is a place of habitation where we are called to enter, actively to respond, sometimes to wrestle, and to dwell in trust as the Spirit teaches us what we need to know.

Assurance

Incline your ear, O LORD, and answer me.

PSALM 86:1

O NE OF THE BEST listeners I have known was a woman who engaged in conversation so generously and with such eagerness that she seemed to listen with her whole body. She leaned in, and seemed to watch as well as listen to one's words as though they were rays of color beaming from a prism. I think of her when I hear the prayer "Incline your ear, O LORD . . .": Bend toward me. Stretch down to meet me in my smallness. Come into intimate space and attend to me. Let the mere whisper that seeps out of my weakness or shame reach you.

The petition is not, however, simply abject. Like so many of the psalmist's prayers, it is grounded in the confidence that when we speak, God does listen — that we can claim the audacity it takes to bring our most intimate concerns before the God of the Universe who does and will "incline" an ear and answer.

Perhaps we have heard these assurances before. The pertinent matter when we make this prayer is what God's answer might look like. The answer to "I want an answer" may well be "You have the answer." To pray honestly for an answer to our prayers is to be willing to recognize and heed the answers we've already been given — in Scripture, in the shared wisdom of our spiritual community, in the examples of other people's lives, in our own deepest intuitions, which are accessible only if we quiet ourselves enough to face our fears, suspend our evasive strategies, and own up to what we already know.

Often in prayer this clear assurance has come to me: "You have what you need." You have the resources, the experience, the willing friends, the memories, the parables and stories that can equip you for this moment: call on them. Prayers are answered in other ways, of course, but this answer is worth particular consideration. It is an answer that wise parents often give children — not "I will come help you," but "You know how to do this; try it."

It may be that what underlies most of our petitions, even the most helpless cries, is a prayer for courage to step out of abject need and trust that, with the help of the Spirit who is always present, we can meet our needs with intelligence and grace — courage to leap out of the boat knowing Christ will meet us on the water.

Some who pray receive a clear directive: "Go." "Give." "Rest." "Let go." "Forgive." "Reframe." Most who pray with an open heart receive the comfort and reassurance that lie in prayer itself, which is the practice of the presence of God. But some receive their answer in a reminder of what God has already given. We don't know what we're being prepared for. We often don't realize that what we're doing is preparation. But it is often the case that the answer we pray for when God inclines an ear is the answer

God was providing all along — an answer that may be, "Look and see what has already been unfolding. What wave is already cresting. What provision has already been made." If we lift our gaze beyond the anxieties, we may see that God has been listening.

Esther also was taken into the king's palace and
put in custody of Hegai, who had charge of the women.

ESTHER 2:8

"Custody" is an unsettling word, associated as it so often is with custody disputes in divorce cases or with crime suspects being taken into custody. Its more benevolent meaning is "protective care or guardianship." It also means "imprisonment." The two meanings often overlap: what passes for care can also be a kind of imprisonment, as it was for Esther, commanded to join the harem of King Ahasuerus, watched over by the king's eunuch, and chosen with no consultation of her wishes as queen of a people not her own. Hegai, the caregiver, was also in custody — given a measure of power, but only on the king's terms. Conversely, imprisonment can be a condition of real care — as one hopes is the case when people who are dangerously mentally ill are committed to a care facility for treatment.

As adults, we may think of ourselves as free and independent agents, but in fact we are "under care." We are in custody. Not only are we dependent upon the various social services that keep us from danger — fire and police departments, for instance — but we are, more significantly, in the kindly custody of friends who tell us truths we need to hear, of families whose need for us is indeed a tie that binds, and, most importantly, of God, who has given the angels charge over us to guide us on our journeys. We are held, beheld, and beholden.

It is partly up to us to determine whether these custodial relationships provide life-giving care or become imprisoning. Esther entered into the service of the king in a spirit of obedience, but also found a way to turn that service to her own God-given purposes. When we find ourselves in work situations that seem entrapping and demand energies we'd rather spend on things that matter more to us, our choices are generally to escape, to capitulate and accept a certain kind of economic slavery, or to work within the "custody" of the institutions, organizations, or corporations from which we make our living. Any of these options may be legitimate and right, at least for a season. Which of them is needful and appropriate is a matter for prayerful discernment — whether it's time to hand in a resignation, trusting that the next thing will emerge, or to negotiate for more livable terms of employment, or to accept what we can't change and find ways, as Esther did, to bring our situation into alignment with our deepest callings.

At some times in all our lives we will be caregivers; at others, cared for. Both of these conditions are callings — custodianship, and living in custody. Each condition carries a cost, and each confers possibilities for creative consent to God's mysterious guidance. We are, finally, in no one's custody but Christ's, whose care is unconditional, whose mercy is greater than we can imagine, and who is waiting for us at the end of whatever road we travel. Slave or free, helper or helpless, saint or stumbling sinner, in life and in death, we are the Lord's.

He . . . fed you in the wilderness with manna. . . .

DEUTERONOMY 8:15-16

At the beginning of a recent worship service, elders handed out pieces of paper and pencils without any mention of what they were for. Midway through the sermon, during which we were invited to reflect on God's provision, even in hard times, the pastor gave us the assignment: "Write your spiritual autobiography in six words." The exercise seemed a little diversionary at first, since I'd come hoping to relax into an inspiring message, but, as with haiku, the radical limitation posed an inviting challenge. I closed my eyes and drew a deep breath, asking that the little exercise not be lost on me, and that whatever words came might be a blessing. The church was quiet. I could hear pencils scratching. In the silence, six words came, perfect in the way they addressed my recurrent anxieties about saving and spending, keeping and letting go, prudent stewardship and the practice of generosity: "Eat the manna. More will come."

It was the way my mother lived — most of her life not far from the edge of poverty, but rich in trust and stories about just the right amount of food, money, help showing up just when it was needed. She was careful about making the dollars stretch to the end of the month, but she also knew when to eat the manna. She knew that some things — most things — are to be used, enjoyed, and shared rather than stored.

Besides being a parable about relying on God's provision, the story of manna in the wilderness is a story about how grace often comes in odd, unsettling, barely recognizable ways. The word "manna," according to some scholars, means "What is it?" God didn't send the Israelites braided challah or fresh salad greens. Their daily "bread" was a strange, flaky substance, something like hoarfrost, that had to be gathered in the morning before it melted in the sun. They molded it into cakes that tasted a little like honey. Some scholars suggest that the word derives from the Arabic words "man hu," meaning "This is plant lice." In fact, certain insects did produce a substance that dried and was eaten in the ancient Middle East. But as the story is told, whatever the biochemistry of manna, the Israelites found it unfamiliar, and had to learn to gather, prepare, and eat it.

It takes time, I find, to recognize that we have what we need when our notion of what we need is confined by habit and expectation. We may not have the money to replace an appliance, but we may have a neighbor who can fix it. We may not have our closest friend nearby when sorrow strikes, but someone may surface from the margins of our lives with a big heart and a listening ear. Solutions may come from unexpected sources. The answer to many prayers, reinforced with every celebration of the Eucharist, is simply this reminder: "You have what you need." Take it. Eat it. There will be more.

. . . for you alone, O LORD, make me dwell in safety.

PSALM 4:8

When our daughter was assailed by nighttime fears and afraid to sleep, we encouraged her to learn this verse by heart. It is hard to know how much that little practice helped at the time, but encouraging her has encouraged me to find in it the help I needed in the midst of sometimes overwhelming fears and anxieties that ranged from schoolyard bullying to urban violence to water contamination to escalating war.

We live not only with new kinds of threats to human safety but with unprecedented awareness of those threats. We're not wired to take in as much information as we now have to process. If we read or listen to the news, our imaginations are stretched sometimes to the breaking point by disasters real and pending around the world. I know people who won't read the papers for that very reason. Though North Americans have had the privilege of feeling "safe" to the degree that they invest trust in a trillion-dollar "national security" program, that illusion has been pretty thoroughly demolished since 9/11.

W. H. Auden wrote a poem during World War II entitled "Leap Before You Look." It begins with the startling line "The sense of danger must not disappear," and ends with "Our dream of safety has to disappear." The poem is an appeal to resist the false innocence or willful ignorance that takes refuge in specious promises of safety. As people of faith, we know, or ought to know, that our safety does not lie in state-of-the-art nuclear weapons or in elaborate airport scanning procedures or in bigger prisons and police forces. The safety we are called to as God's children lies beyond the dangers to life and limb that we all learn to live with, beyond risk assessment, beyond burglar alarms. "You alone, O LORD, make me dwell in safety." We can learn to believe this is true even though God's safety is not always as comfortable a place as a warm room with a locked door.

I once worked with a remarkable woman who had survived three concentration camps after a childhood in the Viennese ghetto. Years later, she wrote a poem called "A Colloquy with the Angel of Death." In a conversation about that poem she made a remark I have remembered many times since: "When you've come face to face with your own death, you are freed from fear of it. You're liberated for life." To be liberated from the fear of death is to be freed unto life — and surely this is a core message of the gospel. We do not need to fear death. Many accounts of near-death experiences echo the same message: those who "cross over" on the operating table or in auto accidents return to tell remarkably similar stories of having experienced a peace more profound than they could have imagined, having come back somewhat reluctantly, and having awakened to a changed sense of what this life is about, and a feeling that they would never again fear death.

God can and does send angels to guard us. People are miraculously healed or saved in this life. And surely it behooves us to work for safe living and working conditions for all who are vulnerable. But many die, many suffer, and many live with a sense of danger that will not disappear any time soon. The good news we can claim and bear is that there is a safety bigger than all the dangers of this world, and that there we have a dwelling place.

... your life is *hidden with Christ* in God.
COLOSSIANS 3:3

My brother and I grew up on our dad's stories. Images of his life before we knew him were as rich and varied for me as actual memories of my own life with him: a six-year-old on a streetcar in 1919; a ten-year-old with conspicuous ears composing a valentine; a boy alone on a pier at San Pedro Harbor "watching the ships come and go"; a naked stowaway washed up on a Manila beach; a journalist hanging around the margins of Hollywood; a GI lurking in London's antiquarian bookshops; a white giant in a pith helmet standing Kiplingesque among a gaggle of Indian children.

My own memories mingle with the stories he made of his — memories that for me go back to being held secure in his arms in a doorway, blinking at the night sky while the house shook and I survived my first earthquake unharmed.

But for all the richness of memory and story, what came to me forcibly in the last weeks of his life was how much remains unknown and unknowable about those we love and think we know. Part of honoring my father at his death was to remember what I knew of him and what he chose to tell, harvesting the gifts,

letting the chaff fly away. Still, in that process I came to recognize
the mystery and hiddenness of that one human life which, like all
lives, had its perplexing incongruities, ragged edges, and incom-
pletions as well as its many moments of goodness and laughter
and invention. Even as it brought to mind a wealth of stories,
Dad's death reminded me that his life and our lives are "hidden
with Christ," and visible here — even at close range — only
through a glass darkly. It was strangely consoling at the time to
realize that only God judges because only God knows his whole
story. Only God fully understands how what looked like pain may
have been blessing, what struggles may have been growth in process, and what particular word of love Dad was created to speak.
It seemed to me a reminder of heaven — the incompletion, the
gaps, the questions we could no longer ask him, the refusal of
his or any life to resolve into a final bright lucidity. Like the dark
side of the moon, part of his story would remain unknown to us,
who would have liked resolution and closure. I felt wistful about
that, but the fact of that finality gave me a new appreciation of
the hope Paul offers in 1 Corinthians 13: what we get in answer
to our deepest desires to understand those we are given to love
is not a fully satisfying exit line, but a promise: "Then we shall
know, even as also we are known."

So *all Israel was recorded in genealogies,* and these
are written in the Book of the Kings of Israel.

1 CHRONICLES 9:1

Though I haven't spent much time on the popular pursuit of family genealogy, I know a number of people who have traced their
ancestors back for ten generations or more, finding in the names
the second and third marriages, the death of infants, the record of
migrations — rich material for reflection on that dimension of
their own identity that has to do with "roots," place, race, class,
genetic conditions, and the ways individuals who were links in a
lineage broke free and, for good or ill, grafted new varieties of fruit
onto the family tree. Imagination fills in the large gaps, weaving a
history like a rag rug from colorful fragments of information.

The function of genealogy in tribal cultures is partly to clar-
ify who belongs to the people, perhaps as much for purposes of
sharing resources equitably as for exclusion. "Membership" still
matters as families and church communities and organizations
stabilize themselves through mutual obligations as well as privi-
leges. That Christians are "members of one Body" is more than
an idea, and even more than a metaphor: it is a spiritual truth that
is meant to trump all other notions of belonging and identity.
We must not let the idea that we are all "children of God" and
"brothers and sisters" fall into cliché and rust there; it may be
one of the most important stays against violence and anarchy.

When I was in college and my faith began to change shape and generate new questions, I found unexpected reassurance in the idea of the "communion of saints." That long lineage of the faithful, those who have gone before us, leaving stories and songs and structures of worship in their wake, provide models and mentors, correctives and incentives to our own spiritual growth. As we discover them, they become ours to claim — part of the genealogy of the family of God in whom we may find our truest belonging. On the walls of many churches — close to my home, for instance, in the sanctuary of Our Lady of the Angels in Los Angeles and in the rotunda of St. Gregory of Nyssa in San Francisco — figures and faces of saints, known and less known, provide a visible reminder of the ranks of those who still uphold us on our earthly journeys. They are our people — ours to turn to for learning and comfort and example.

T. S. Eliot, writing in *Little Gidding* of his own pilgrimage to an ancestral chapel, reminds himself, "You are here to kneel/where prayer has been valid." Others have prayed before us, and their prayers have opened the paths we tread. May our prayers do the same for the small ones for whom even now we make room in the great circle of grace.

... but his *delight is in the law* of the LORD. . . .

PSALM 1:2

Years ago a young orthodox rabbi visited the high school where I was teaching. As requested, he explained for a religious studies class some of the many laws he and other practicing Jews were expected to keep. As he moved from laws regulating Sabbath activities to kosher laws to laws regarding sex and social behavior, the students grew increasingly incredulous. Finally one of the bolder ones asked, genuinely curious, "How can you stand living with all those laws?" The rabbi's answer was memorable. First he smiled. Then he said, "The law is like a fence that protects a safe space for us to be at home in. It's like the walls of a house that shelters us and gives us a home designed for our needs. We consider it a great gift." Clearly he loved the law in something like the way David did. Though Jesus challenged simplistic applications of the law, and brought news of grace that frees us from the law, he did not, he insisted, come to abolish it.

There is still delight to be had in law, particularly since we are not slaves to it. A good law preserves kinds of order that serve the whole community. A good law protects justice, even though no law can insure it. A good law is adaptable to the shifting circumstances of an evolving culture — sturdy, but malleable enough to allow for new interpretations as times change. Though much of what we learned in American history textbooks has seemed to me in later life a biased and troubling narrative in which the points of view of the oppressed have been under- or misrepresented, I still find myself amazed at the wisdom and prescience of the makers of the American Constitution. Though it has been tugged at and amended and disputed, it has held like a well-engineered building through the political storms and earthquakes of these many decades, and provides us with a good example of the kind of law for which one may well feel gratitude and delight.

The law of God, written in Scripture and on our hearts, has certainly been a matter of much greater and longer dispute, and has of late been invoked for a variety of questionable political purposes, but this core truth still seems to me cause for delight: God gives us guidance, opening a path before us and providing directions for the journey, calling us into interpretive communities where we may be held gently accountable, and meeting us at that journey's end. Sought and lived into and loved, embodied in the One who is the Way, the Truth, and the Light, divine law does not constrain us, but sets us free indeed, to dance before the altar and walk confidently on our daily paths with deepening delight.

Make me to know your ways, O LORD; *teach me your paths.*
PSALM 25:4

Yosemite National Park publishes a newsprint guide for visitors that lists a bewildering range of activities for eager tourists. Many of these are hikes, some led by a ranger. The paths that wind through this magnificent mountain country are many, some challenging for even veteran hikers, some accessible for nearly all comers. They are well marked and maintained, cuts in funding to national parks notwithstanding. All the trails have names. Thousands of travelers make annual pilgrimages to the park to hike their favorite trails yet again, where familiar pine scents, the red bark of manzanita bushes, and occasional stands of ancient ferns welcome them back to deeply refreshing contact with a precious spot of earth. They know those paths.

Learning a path is a long, patient process. A friend of ours has hiked the same trail near his home once or twice a week for many years. Other trails thread the nearby hills, and he travels them when invited, but the trail he knows and loves is *his;* he has a claim on it that can be won only by long, patient, appreciative intimacy. He knows every patch of shade, where the sounds of water become audible, which parts get muddy first in the January rain. He knows it in ways that go far beyond navigation. His path has become a way of knowing himself. The stretch of solitude it allows him enables and shapes the ongoing conversation with himself that has furnished his "interior castle."

Another friend, similar in his fidelity to places he has traveled on foot, made a months-long spiritual exercise out of clearing a trail around the perimeter and along the streambeds on the wooded campus where he works. He moved sizeable rocks, protected obtrusive tree roots, trimmed back poison oak, and thought, as he worked, about the refuge this rustic walkway might provide not only for him after a day of classes and committees, but for anyone who needed a little time away from the noise and haste. The Japanese call it *"Shinrin-yoku"* — forest bathing — the renewing time one spends among the quiet living things who are our fellow creatures.

When the psalmist prays, "Make me to know your ways, O LORD; teach me your paths," I imagine he is asking for something more than a map: what he seeks is a lived relationship with the shepherd who knows every cranny of the hills, and will accompany him as he explores — and plays in — the fields of the Lord. This is the same poet who sang with radical confidence, "though I walk through the valley of the shadow of death, I will fear no evil, for you are with me. . . ." As Jesus walked the paths of Nazareth and Jerusalem and the hills of Samaria, teaching his disciples how to be at home among the foxes and the birds of the air and the hungry crowds of strangers, so our teacher walks with us. The Spirit will meet us, even on our detours and byways, even in the pits we stumble into, and will teach us, step by step, how to recognize and walk the paths of this world as the many roads to heaven they are. On them, as the poet Theodore Roethke put it in "The Waking," we can walk in trust and "learn by going" where we have to go.

I bless the LORD who gives me counsel;
in the night also my heart instructs me.
PSALM 16:7

Again and again in biblical stories God offers guidance in dreams: he warns Abimelech; he directs Jacob and offers him a vision of angels; he instructs Laban; he gives Joseph foreknowledge of his ascent to power and makes him an interpreter of others' dreams, as he also does Daniel; he foretells military success for Gideon by means of another man's dream; he summons Solomon to prayer; he challenges Job; he reassures Joseph that he should take the pregnant Mary as his wife, warns him to flee Herod, and summons him back from Egypt. Though there are also numerous warnings, especially in the book of Jeremiah, about the dangers of dreamers who make false claims, it is clear that the power of dreams, and the value of the information they can convey, are to be taken seriously. The Talmud goes so far as to say, "A dream that has not been interpreted is like a letter that has not been opened."

What comes to us in the night, sleeping or waking, comes through different channels from those illumined by the rational light of day. As the psalmist puts it, "In the night also my heart instructs me." In the night our minds wander and fade, and matters of the heart — our anxieties, our hopes, our grieving, our affections — may either keep us awake or find their way into the inner places where dreams are made. What we know in our hearts is often obscured or overruled by our minds, and our intuitions are silenced by calculation or judged and dismissed because they don't make waking "sense."

Dreams speak symbolically. Though they may invite and instruct, direct and sometimes foretell, they do so in ways that demand imaginative, thoughtful, and sometimes courageous interpretation: they may reveal what we have kept carefully hidden from ourselves or summon us to costly enterprises we wouldn't have chosen. The work of interpreting dreams takes skill and requires some instruction from those who have devoted time, attention, and prayer to these curious instruments of awareness; they are easily underestimated and easily misunderstood. It is a business that deserves to be undertaken prayerfully: we ask that what guidance is available in the images of a dream may open our understanding and our hearts to God's purposes.

The archetypes that appear in dreams may have different levels of meaning, and may yield different dimensions of meaning on longer-term reflection. A dream about swimming in the ocean may be about trust, or about the depth and danger of an undertaking, or about learning what writer Elizabeth O'Connor called "the wisdom of insecurity." A dream about being given a key might be a call to take an action one has been avoiding, to open a door and walk across a threshold that will lead to uncertainty and change. Or it might be a reassurance that you have in your hands what you need to make an important decision or transition. Dreams remind us that we do not live by reason alone; that the Creator has made us fearfully and wonderfully capable of intuitive leaps, gut feelings and wild guesses, metaphor and imagination. Those gifts are ours to claim, and to use for our own and others' instruction, and to welcome as one of the ways in which God, who works in mysterious ways, gives us counsel.

I will *make a way* in the wilderness and rivers in the desert.

ISAIAH 43:19

Some time ago our son spent a season building and maintaining trails in the mountains of the Southwest with AmeriCorps. It was arduous work. It involved moving rocks and dirt, clearing brush, and considering how to accommodate human traffic without damaging the life forms that dwelt in those high deserts. Making a way in the wilderness puts humans in new relationship to the wilderness, bringing us closer to its beauties and dangers and, because it disrupts growth patterns and microhabitats, requiring more conscious interaction with the places we have entered. A new pathway brings new responsibilities.

The parting of the Red Sea, perhaps the most dramatic instance of God's "making a way," is a forceful intervention: tons of sea water held at bay by a preternatural and unpredictable force must have been a prospect almost as threatening as the Egyptian armies that pursued the fleeing Israelites. This being the only option, they took it, but it has often struck me in reading that story (and, no doubt, referencing the visual image of Charlton Heston leading the ragged lines of escapees into those depths in the 1956 film *The Ten Commandments*) that most of them must have been looking around for some other way, since the way the Lord had made looked almost as daunting as the death or captivity that threatened from behind.

"Where there is a will, there is a way." The implications of this familiar bit of folk wisdom become more complicated when the will in question is God's. Though God speaks at times in a still small voice rather than the mighty whirlwind, the repertoire of divine strategies certainly includes earthquake, fire, flood, and mighty winds. God opens paths that invite, but almost always the invitation entails a challenge: set your foot on the path and do not look back. Go with no map but a promise. Enter the unknown. A beautiful line from one of Wendell Berry's poems in *A Timbered*

Choir suggests how we are to do that: "I go amazed/into the maze of a design/that mind can follow, but not know. . . ."

The kind of journey God may invite us to is also beautifully represented in Tolkien's great journey parable, *The Fellowship of the Ring*, when Frodo — small, home-loving, disinclined to an adventure riddled with uncertainties — steps up to the call of the moment and, like David before Goliath, makes his consequential offer: "I will take the ring, though I do not know the way." The forces that clear a way through alien territories for the hobbit and his little band are beyond his reckoning, but he knows enough to trust in Gandalf's power and Aragorn's experience and Sam's fidelity and the hospitality of strangers along the long road through Middle Earth. His guidance comes not from a map or a plan, but from relationships of trust.

Jesus' mysterious claim "I am the Way" radically reorganizes our notions of what it may mean for God to "make a way" for us. Direction will apparently come on a "need-to-know" basis, in relationship. Our job is to stay in relationship, not to carry a topo map. There isn't one. The ground may shift. The Way lies in holding the gaze of the one who renews the invitation moment by moment: "Follow me." As we do that, though we may tread on the asp and the viper, we will also be held by a power stronger than geomagnetism and a clarity sharper than the clearest line on a map as we enter unknown territory following a will whose purposes we can't fathom into territory we don't yet know on the strength of a promise whose fulfillment is no guarantee of safety or comfort in this world, but offers us abundant life and light in the darkness that has not, and cannot, overcome it.

A third part of you . . . *I will scatter* to all the winds. . . .

EZEKIEL 5:12

Repeated twice among the dire threats of punishment directed to a recalcitrant and rebellious people is this one — that a third of the community will be scattered to the winds. Scattering is a curse, as gathering is a blessing; the flip side of this threat is a promise. Though some may be called to the hermit's life, generally we were not meant to live alone, but thrive best in community. We need one another; we need the complementary skills and corrective gazes and support and sympathy and loving kindness that no one of us can manufacture for ourselves. "Stay together," we tell young people on urban field trips or excursions into the wilderness. "Come stay with us," we tell widows in time of loss or friends who have lost homes to fire or flood. We gather over Thanksgiving dinners and around birthday cakes. "Shall we gather by the river . . ." we sing, swaying to guitars as we renew our shared hope in song. Recent natural disasters have driven the most diverse communities and even leaders of conflicting political persuasions to "pull together" and reconsider the common good in a more generous light. In hard times we see more clearly how we need each other. Isolation in those times is not only hard, but often life-threatening.

But the ways in which we need each other are often obscured for those of us who live in a culture where mobility is expected and required for many jobs, individualism is elevated to an ethic, and independence is presumed to be a core value in early childhood training. American national mythology glorifies the loner who "lights out for the territory," rejecting the constraints of civilizing aunts and domestic duties. Today we depend for many of our material needs on people we don't know and often participate in oppression, supporting sweatshop labor as we buy our cheaply made, expensively marketed clothing. Indeed, we too easily develop a vested interest in ignoring the plight of laborers, since to recognize it would convict us of our collective guilt. The sheer scale on which business is conducted and travel undertaken makes it hard to hang onto a sense of the "village" it takes to raise a child or the truth of adages like "We're all in it together," or a sense of who is my neighbor. Anonymity is not only inevitable; it has become, for many of us, normative. We don't expect — or even want — to be recognized in the middle of the city, and so our sense of accountability shrinks. We are a scattered people.

Gathering, therefore — building and fostering community — requires prayerful attention. Ultimately, real community is a gift from the Spirit who directs our ways, but sustaining community is a sacred, human, often demanding task. To gather — for worship or prayer, or around a bereaved family, or in a hospital room, or where free lunches are served to the homeless — we have to lay aside the personal occupations that keep us closely focused in our own homes, traveling our daily routes, caring for our nuclear families. It requires a wide, even global look at the challenges we face together — climate change, water shortages, pollution, hunger, disease — and at the deep theological truths that give us hope even in a time like this: that God is with us, a very present help in time of trouble, that we are each other's brothers and sisters, that our life together as members of one Body is guided and directed by the "Master of Surprises," who teaches us again and again that our calling in this world is to be channels of grace for one another anywhere two or three are gathered.

Therefore a man shall leave his father and his mother
and hold fast to his wife, and the two shall *become one flesh.*
GENESIS 2:24

What does it mean to be "one flesh"? That word, "flesh," is pretty intrusive when uttered, as it so often is, in a context of white veils and hymns and love poetry. Lest we be tempted to over-spiritualize matrimony, we are reminded in the very beginning of Genesis that we are fleshly creatures with fleshly appetites, that the terms on which we unite with one another in this life — in shared meals, in the shared marriage bed, and even in the shared sacrament of the Lord's Supper — are incarnational. Our bodies are sources of pleasure, knowledge, and mystery for one another. They're also the sites where we are tested and taught by sickness, weariness, physical limits, and, finally, death. Loving one another, we love what is mortal.

Jesus' miracles affirmed the goodness of our fleshly lives. He spat in the mud and healed a blind man. He raised a child from her deathbed and said, "Give her something to eat." He made wine for the pleasure of wedding guests in Cana and held children on his lap. And in his own flesh he grew weary and wept, dripped sweat and bled. Every Sunday we proclaim our belief in the resurrection of the body — another of those mysteries about which believers speculate, sometimes to the point of bitter quarrels, but a mystery that is, it seems to me, profoundly comforting and healthily different from any spirituality that denies the luminous loveliness and intricacy of the body.

From our bodies we learn our first and deepest dependencies and pleasures, our capacity to leap for joy and curl close around our sorrow, the language of touch that serves where words leave off. They are agents of intelligence and empathy that connect us with the rest of creation. Through them we receive, as Mary Oliver puts it in "The Plum Trees," richness that is "carried inward on the five/rivers!" "Joy is a taste," she says, "before/it's anything else," echoing the psalmist's cry, "O taste and see that the Lord is good!" Our bodies are precious gifts, entrusted to each other in friendships and families as well as, more intimately, in marriage, to care for in this life with humility and thanksgiving.

I love the story of the abbot who, when a young monk came to him dismayed and said, "Father, I can't go to Mass; I'm so mired in doubt, I'm afraid I've lost my faith," replied, "Then come with my faith." That trust in the love that allows us to step in and pinch-hit for each other, take each other's place, stand in each other's shoes, and hold each other up is anchored deeply in the life of the body where we first learn about being held, shielded, stretched, and wrestled with.

24

In *Brideshead Revisited*, Evelyn Waugh claimed that to love one human being is the root of wisdom. The love of human beings begins in the "humus" or soil we are made of — those six elements — oxygen, carbon, hydrogen, nitrogen, calcium, and phosphorus — the "too, too solid flesh" that is sometimes a burden and sometimes a source of surpassing delight. Paul's image of believers as members of one body goes well beyond metaphor; as embodied beings we are made of this earth, for each other, breathed into and called forth to participate in "the life of significant soil." Becoming "one flesh" has particular meaning with reference to marriage, where flesh meets flesh in a unique way. But in a broader way worth claiming, we who are "one in the Spirit" are also one in the soil, and in the water that courses through us and the air that fills our lungs and the DNA that differs, between your body and mine, only in a few very minute particulars.

In him *we live and move and have our being.*
ACTS 17:28

This lovely triad is among the most poetic and comprehensive ways of describing our relationship to God. The three terms seem a little redundant at first — living and moving and having our being in God are all ways of saying that the God "whose center is everywhere and whose periphery is nowhere" surrounds and upholds and sustains us. But each term offers its own invitation to imagine the intimacy God offers us.

We live in him the way we live in the air that surrounds us. God is our dwelling place, our home, the place toward which all our wanderings tend. God is the source of our breath and bodies, of the dust of which we are made. God is spacious; in him we move like a dancer on a stage or a swimmer who dives beneath the waves and surfaces, rejoicing in the elements of earth, air, and water, in turn.

In God we are held close and safe, and from that place of safety we reach into the known and unknown world with the energy and appetite that love provides. There is nowhere to "flee from his presence," because God meets us, or, as T. S. Eliot puts it, "prevents us" everywhere.

We move in him as through the seasons, discovering and re-discovering forms of beauty that come and go and come again, all aspects of one life living itself, in which we have our share. Space and time unscroll into story, and every story rings changes on the original unfolding of love into light into song. We move as readers and participants through the vast, unfolding story of salvation, inhabiting that story as we pause over words, allow images their impact on our imaginations, and illustrate and enliven the archetypes it provides with instances from our own lives. The older we get, the more memory informs our reading of Scripture, and the more its wisdom becomes specifically, personally, assuringly available.

Our very beings — our way of being in the world, the way we situate ourselves in our families, among our friends, the personality traits we develop, the cultural habits we appropriate — are modified to the extent that we practice the presence of God. In that divine light everything looks different; we are permeated to translucency when we allow ourselves to be indwelt by the Light from Light, whose robe is the light, and who is in very fact the Light of the World. "I in God, God in me" is one of the deep paradoxes mystics speak about with an intimacy that can be only partially expressed in language. So they resort to the language of sexual union, or sometimes of water, air, and sunlight to find a way to speak truly about the deep interpenetration of God and human that is enacted each time we receive the Eucharist, recognizing that the God who made the galaxies made of those same elements the dirt, the wheat, the bread, and the body that is fed, and that God consents to enter into our very bodies and selves and into the intricacy of protein manufacture and cell division to meet us in our human condition. We are made of this earth, made of the rich dirt of which this earth is made, made by the One who enlivens every neuron, through whom all things were made, and without whom was not anything made that was made.

Invitation and Admonition

For he will *speak peace* to his people. . . .

PSALM 85:8

PEACE IS A LANGUAGE. To "speak peace" is very different from speaking *of* peace. To speak *of* peace is to reason about it. But to speak peace is to impart it. The promise in this psalm is that God will make peace with us and among us. But the phrase also serves as a reminder that our words are acts. When we speak, we may stir up animosities, suspicions, jealousies, or old hurts — or we may impart peace.

Peace may be "uttered" not only in gentleness of voice when we speak, but in the choice of words that reframe, redirect, or surprise us into reconsidering. Sometimes a way of describing the problem or conflict as an opportunity for invention or imagination or learning can enable those who are stuck in a point of view to see a new way.

To speak peace might be to pose a question that gives pause. Are you willing to endanger friendship to have it your way? Would you rather be right than be in relationship? What might mutual satisfaction look like? How much of your emotional energy are you expending on this conflict? Where would you rather spend those precious resources? Do you want an opinion or an affirmation? What is the need that fuels your argument?

Systematic approaches to nonviolent communication like Marshall Rosenberg's have been widely taught and used successfully to help resolve serious public and political conflicts as well as personal ones. The principles are simple: all human beings share the same basic needs; all negotiations are attempts to meet needs; feelings indicate needs being met or unmet; human beings can change. Holding compassion as a core intention underlies all the ideas that inform this method of peacemaking.

Methods vary, but compassion remains the heart of peacemaking. It is what has enabled families in South Africa whose sons have been murdered to forgive, and even foster relationship with the murderer. It is what has enabled members of warring ethnic groups in Iraq to gather, at some risk, in public places to recite poetry together. It is what has brought Protestants and Catholics in Northern Ireland into open-hearted conversation, even as street fighting continued.

If we are to speak peace, our speaking must be an extension of prayer. If we ask to be made "channels of peace," as in the beautiful prayer of St. Francis, we offer ourselves in that request as conduits of God's own healing energy to those we encounter, and ask that our words become instruments of grace.

Speech has a high place in the biblical story. God's speaking brought all things into being. Our words, carried on the breath of life, in small but sacramental ways bring about change in the world around us. Conversation, a word that once meant "to walk with" or "to dwell with," is where peacemaking can grow roots that anchor action.

Silence provides a context for such conversation. In a world of noise, silence requires deliberate intention and preparation; we have to seek it out, or find ways to create it. God speaks into our silences. If we are to speak peace and be heard, we must first listen into the silence that allows prayer to happen and into the silences that allow others to breathe and soften and open their hearts in our presence. In a pool of silence, words can open like water lilies and assume new patterns of meaning.

"Peace comes dropping slow," Yeats wrote, "dropping from the veils of the morning to where the cricket sings." So may words of peace slow to the beat of a calm heart and drop into moments of daily life like dew — subtle, quiet, and life-giving, without fanfare or even announcement, like a fragrance.

May our peacemaking begin in heartbeats attuned to the rhythms of the Spirit who dwells in us and sustains the breath of which our words are made.

You shall not *make for yourself a carved image, or any likeness*
of anything that is in heaven above, or that is in the earth
beneath, or that is in the water under the earth.

EXODUS 20:4

It seems a little too easy to breeze past the Second Commandment, which appears primarily to be an admonishment to the
troublesome lot of ancient rabble who melted gold into a calf
and prayed to it. Quaint, primitive behavior, inapplicable to us
who are far too self-aware and sophisticated to pray to idols.
Even when we are rightly reminded that our materialism is a form
of idolatry, I wonder if we miss a dimension of warning in this
sweeping prohibition.

No generation or culture has made more images than this one.
We can digitize everything from subatomic particles to the rings
of Saturn. In an effort to "capture the moment," we whip out our
cameras and make our own likenesses of things in heaven and on
earth. But (one may object) we don't worship those images. And
we don't, exactly. Still, I wonder to what extent we do allow our
affections, our desires, our memories, and even our spiritual lives
to be shaped by the images we make.

Photography is so pervasive — and so useful, if we think of
its applications in medicine, education, and journalism, to name
a few — it is hard to consider the insidious ways we might be led
astray by our own image-making.

In C. S. Lewis's *Perelandra*, a story about two humans who travel to another planet, one to bring about the Fall, the other to try to prevent it, the tempter, a profit-driven scientist named Weston, shows the still-innocent Eve figure her own image in a mirror. "We call this thing a mirror," he explains. "A man can love himself, and be together with himself. That is what it means to be a man or a woman — to walk alongside oneself as if one were a second person and to delight in one's own beauty. Mirrors were made to teach this art." "Is it a good?" the Lady asks. Ransom, the other human, answers quickly with an emphatic "No." It is the same answer to which we are led by the ancient myth of Narcissus, who, captivated by his own image, fell into the water and drowned.

I have seen small children lose something of their innocence in the course of posing for pictures: as they open presents, hug their puppies, or dress for first communion, they are stopped, snapped, and then shown their own images. They learn to manufacture performance smiles, and to love their beautiful selves from outside in. Though I do take pictures on occasion, and enjoy them, I wonder what are the moral limits to this commonplace pleasure.

The protagonist of Hawthorne's 1851 novel *The House of the Seven Gables* is a daguerrotypist, aptly named Holgrave, who practices the new art of "photogravure." This art, which involves "capturing light" and making it into images, is represented as, and unsettlingly like, wizardry or witchcraft. It has the power to fascinate and, literally, to divert. The question implicitly posed in that story is worth raising: From what are we diverting ourselves with our much making of images? It is, I suppose, a very Protestant question that could lead down another winding path to thoughtless iconoclasm. I don't want to follow that path very far; I love Michelangelo's Pietà and Donatello's Magdalene and Fra Angelico's angels and my parents' wedding portrait and certain sweet shots of children. Still, the value of images in church windows or on our bedroom dressers deserves some personal and communal reflection.

Susan Sontag's edgy essay "The Image-World" makes the point with no apologies: "The possession of a camera can inspire something akin to lust. And like all credible forms of lust, it cannot be satisfied: first, because the possibilities of photography are infinite, and, second, because the project is finally self-devouring. The attempts by photographers to bolster up a depleted sense of reality contribute to the depletion." That "sense of reality" is worth protecting from the erosion of images that commercialize or trivialize or romanticize what we need to see with eyes of love and critical intelligence. Who we are is a question best answered by looking into the eyes of those who look back, and sometimes by closing our eyes altogether, breathing deep, and dwelling safe simply in the knowledge that we are known.

I will *pray to the* LORD *for you.*
1 SAMUEL 7:5

Intercessory prayer has always puzzled me. I have engaged in it from my earliest childhood when I prayed at bedtime for people who were sad or poor or sick. And I have never stopped believing that it's a good thing to do. But my understanding of what it means to pray *for* has taken a number of turns.

I am very likely not the only one who has found herself wondering what the point might be of naming a particular person and her particular needs to God, who knows and loves her better than I. At one of those moments, finding myself falling into a slightly cynical lethargy about the business of praying for a person whose healing was in any case unlikely, I suddenly had one of those epiphanies that intrude upon us as gifts from a persistent angel — sometimes more like a blow to the head than a shaft of light. I realized there was a significant difference between praying *on behalf of* someone and praying *in someone's stead.* Both matter: interceding for someone too sick or angry or mired in unbelief to pray, directing divine energy in his or her direction, so to speak, speaking up for him or her, is a way of reminding ourselves that we are members of one body, and have both the right and the duty to speak up on behalf of each other for our mutual health. But in this instance, I felt specifically called to pray in someone's stead. Since he could not, and in any event likely would not, pray for himself, I asked God to let me "sub" for him. Let me stand here in his place. Hear my prayer as his prayer.

Somehow the idea that we could "sub" for each other reinvigorated my interest in intercessory prayer. I felt empowered, as a member of one great body, to move like a messenger hormone to the place that needed healing and be there. I felt empowered, in a way still not fully explicable, to *be* the person for whom I was praying.

I had a memorable chance to exercise just that role when a friend whose spouse was dying said, "I can't pray anymore. You're going to have to do it for me." His simple, clear faith that others could take up the work of prayer — *his* prayer — when he could no longer bear it seemed to me then, and seems now, a reminder of what a privilege it is to serve one another in that way.

When Samuel promises to pray to the Lord for Israel, he is assuming an explicitly priestly function of intercession. He offers the burnt offering, and presents the people's case and their need. When we pray for one another, we exercise the priesthood of all believers. That priesthood is a remarkable empowerment and promise that, even when we cannot pray on our own behalf — or when we can't even manage to show up — our brothers and sisters can step in for us and speak on our behalf, in our stead, partners on the journey and proxies before the Judge who is more merciful than we can imagine.

... neither eating bread nor drinking water,
for he was *mourning over the faithlessness* of the exiles. ...
EZRA 10:6

Ezra's response to the moral squalor of his people was to mourn. He took their shame personally. He wept. He cast himself down. He identified with the people whose sins he lamented, and joined them in repentance. Theirs was not an individualistic culture: like collective rejoicing over victories or good harvests, collective shame was real and acute.

I wonder whether, in my sorrow *over* certain egregious offenses

— against fellow humans in specious, for-profit wars, against the earth in rapacious deforestation and ocean pollution, against the poor in policies that drive them into desperation — I am sorry enough *for* those offenses. I wonder if I take stock often enough of the ways I participate in the very sins I deplore, protest, and — to be honest — judge. It is easy, since ours is an individualistic culture, to stand apart from those I regard as warmongers, profiteers, exploiters, deceivers, and oppressors and exercise my moral outrage. To a point, it seems right, still, to "rage against the machine" and all those who operate it. But at some point it behooves me to mourn not only as a witness, but as a penitent co-conspirator.

Mourning comes not from a place of separation, but from a place of solidarity with fellow sinners. Mourning includes personal sorrow over what might have been done differently — over the ways I support what I know to be harmful when I buy, vote, drive, eat, or speak. I am a participant in the very processes that erode justice, mercy, and humility. Even as I try to withdraw my participation, to act with clearer intention, to forgo or boycott destructive products and practices, I have to recognize that as a "rich Christian in an age of hunger" (to use Ron Sider's convicting phrase) and a taxpayer in a military machine, I need to maintain an attitude of repentance, a determination to help change what I can, and a will to look deeply and steadily into what is painful and complicated in order to participate in what heals.

Even to pray well requires that willingness not to avert my gaze from what is shameful to recognize about North American greed, about corruption of food systems, about the hard decisions the working poor have to make every day. That means identifying with the victims and standing with them, but also, paradoxically, recognizing the ways I am aligned with the oppressors, repenting on my own and their behalf, and bringing my politics deep into my prayer life as a sinner participating in sinful systems, a member of a faithless crowd of confused followers not unlike the wandering Israelites, and a hopeful recipient of God's infinite mercy. Humility demands that I seek that mercy not only for myself, but for those I imagine to be most guilty.

I'm old enough to remember the Pogo cartoon with a caption that became a popular bumper sticker during the Vietnam war: "We have met the enemy and he is us." If that is true, then mourning is an important stage of repentance and change: mourning for our own lost innocence, for our unwitting collaboration, for those harmed, for things done and left undone, and, as T. S. Eliot put it, "things ill done, or done to others' harm, which once you took for exercise of virtue."

And you shall not strip your vineyard bare,
neither shall you gather the fallen grapes of your vineyard.
You shall *leave them for the poor* and for the sojourner. . . .
LEVITICUS 19:10

In the context of current public debate, the term "entitlement" is often used skeptically or dismissively to suggest that the tax breaks, welfare checks, Medicaid coverage, and other allowances for the poorest among us somehow reduce individuals' incentives to take responsibility for their own well-being. The debate is ancient, not just current: "What is the responsibility of the state or the wider community toward those who can't or don't care for themselves?" is a question that has vexed those involved in governance since before the Roman Empire. The Israelites, however, enjoyed a certain clarity on the matter. The poor *were* entitled. A portion of the harvest was to be left for them to glean. A place at the table was to be offered.

And Jesus raised the bar even higher, suggesting that we give our cloaks along with our coats to those who asked, and practice a generosity that went way beyond the bounds of duty. One of America's largest organizations committed to feeding the hungry, Feeding America (once called America's Second Harvest), offers these simple, clear statements of commitment in their mission statement (on their Web site):

We honor the lives, concerns, and stories of people in need. . . .

We keep faith with the public trust through the efficient and compassionate use of resources entrusted to us. . . .

We operate with an acute sense of urgency that reflects the immediate needs of people struggling with hunger.

Their methods include contracting with food growers to "capture fresh produce at an earlier stage in the supply chain that translates into increased freshness" and to distribute this produce through food banks. Similar efforts are being pursued in almost every denomination and in the Interfaith Hunger Initiative, which runs "Gleaners' Food Bank." Besides taking encouragement from these widespread efforts, which sidestep political invective by fidelity to simple, sustained direct action, all these groups have in common a commitment to a relational understanding of "entitlement." All who share the planet, most believe, are entitled to basic necessities — and beyond that, to the hospitality of those whose privilege it is to extend it. Feeding America's explicit intent to honor the stories of the poor is a key element in honoring the people themselves. "Who are you?" humanizes and makes more tolerable the question that so often proceeds from a position of power: "What do you need?"

What the poor need is a share, a start, a place to rest, a conversation. The many of us who no longer cultivate fields can still leave a portion for the poor to glean and need, I think, to hang onto that antique verb as a reminder that what we "have" — even what we worked for — is not ours alone. A portion is for the poor, and not because we are generous, but because they are entitled.

Give your servant therefore an understanding mind
to govern your people, *that I may discern* between good and evil,
for who is able to govern this your great people?
1 KINGS 3:9

Solomon's prayer for discernment is one I would commend to every person in a position of leadership. The Latin root means "to separate, sift, or pull apart." The word itself reminds us that the moral ground we stand on is overgrown and entangled, and that right thinking and right action require the patience to pull apart the strands of another's argument or our own, separating what is true and reliable from hearsay, inference, speculation, and deception — a patience that seems increasingly rare when elections or economic pressures sweep us up in a rush to the finish line or the bottom line. Jesus' metaphor clarified the task of discernment: wheat and weeds grow together in the same field. If you pull up one, you may damage the other, so the wise farmer lets them both mature, and then separates them. Discernment has to do not just with the wisdom to distinguish what is good, wise, just, relevant, applicable, or life-giving for the community one serves, but also with what is timely, and what is, for a time, to be tolerated.

The prayer for discernment seems to me one to be said daily by any of us who anticipate that the day will bring us face to face with others' needs, hopes, and agendas. It is a prayer for attunement to the still, small voice that can give us answers when questions arise. Is this a time to say yes and lay aside my own plans? Is this a time to reframe my purposes? Is this a time to say no in order to be true to a deeper yes? Is this a time to pause for reflection, or a time to act decisively, trusting the intuitions that may be the Spirit's best instrument? What claims on my attention, time, and resources deserve most to be honored in this situation? What is the call of the moment?

Discernment seems always to involve willingness to reconsider. If our moral code is set on automatic like cruise control, our judgments become reflexive rather than reflective, rigid rather than responsive. The older I get, the more persuaded I am of the wisdom of the adage "Never say never." Though there are absolutes, they seem to lie at the edges of the great gray area most of us inhabit, where ambiguities, competing goods, and unpredictable outcomes complicate our judgments. We all know the extreme examples from Moral Philosophy 101. Is it right to steal bread to feed a hungry child? Is it right to lie to keep someone from unjust arrest? Is it right to break a law if the law is biased toward the interests of a privileged group? Our daily occasions for discernment may be subtler and seem less consequential than those, but surely they are what give us our training in listening for divine guidance and attuning ourselves to the law written on our hearts and anchored in love of God and neighbor.

Solomon asks not for a moral code — he has the Ten Commandments and all the Levitical laws for the general guidance and protection of his people — but for an understanding mind, that he may discern between good and evil. He needs a good eye and an intelligent ear because good and evil so often look and sound alike. Our tendency to stereotype the "enemy," and to polarize arguments, politics, and parties into two sides rather than recognizing the multiplicity of plausible points of view and the partial merit in most of them comes, I think, from fear. As we attempt to decide on a course of action, it's much more strenuous to consider the context, the mitigating circumstances, the stories of those involved in a messy situation, the competing needs, the levels of complicity, and our own vested interests rather than to cite a law, apply a prescribed fine, and go on to the golf game.

Some things are evil. Some are good. Sometimes it is evident which is which. But most of the time, as journalist Ellen Goodman once said, "The bottom line is always 'It's not that simple.'" We need divine help — the nudging of the Spirit, the sacred stories, the practice of the presence of God in the very midst of things — to choose, and keep choosing, despite all that remains unresolved, the better way.

Blessed is the one who *considers the poor!*
PSALM 41:1

A certain lively compassion is built into the verb "consider." It goes beyond looking or noticing. It means "to look at closely" or "observe." Some linguists link it to an old English word meaning "to stretch or extend," which would imply that when we consider others, we extend ourselves toward them, reaching out with our energies, intentions, arms ready to lift the weary and carry them a while. Other meanings of that old English word include "to dwell long upon." The compassionate gaze of one who considers the poor lingers, takes in their situation, their stories, the social context in which their poverty is rooted, their particular, immediate needs. To look at the person on the street corner in this way, or the disheveled young mother in the Goodwill store trying to find usable baby equipment, or the sullen kids on street corners in the inner city who may be hanging out there to avoid the sounds of domestic violence at home is to be willing to imagine the terms on which they navigate lives made unusually difficult by policies and systems that, for all our righteous public rhetoric, still privilege the privileged.

Some linguists link the root of "consider" to observing the stars, assuming a navigational metaphor based on *sidus* (Latin for "constellation"). Though this word lineage is disputed, it is worth — well — considering: to look at the poor as a sailor looks at the stars is to see them as guides and markers that help us to locate ourselves and define our journey. The poor, as Jesus reminds us, are always with us. This is not a dismissive observation, but a reminder: If we are among those blessed with material abundance, it is the poor who remind us that all we have is given us to share. They mirror and embody one form of poverty that may remind us of another. In considering them — dwelling among them, seeking to understand their plight and the systems in which they are entrapped, seeking justice for them, identifying with them — we find our own way.

Our own way is inseparable from theirs. Our spiritual health is linked to theirs. The idea of the "common good" is not simply an invention of Enlightenment philosophers, but a matter of common sense manifested in ancient practices like leaving the corners of fields for the poor to glean, or practicing debt forgiveness in jubilee years. If a portion of the community fails to thrive, the whole community suffers — sometimes subtly, sometimes in obvious ways like outbreaks of violence born of desperation. When we consider the poor, we connect those dots. We are slow to judge and quick to inquire. We imagine and identify and organize to help remedy the conditions that create the kinds of poverty that diminish us all. When we do that, as Portia elegantly put it, we exercise a quality of mercy that "blesses him that gives and him that takes."

... and *no one spoke a word to him,* for they saw
that his suffering was very great.

JOB 2:13

When they hear of Job's great misfortune, the first response of
his notorious comforters — Eliphaz, Bildad, and Zophar — is
admirable: they gather together and decide to go comfort him.
When they see him, they're shocked. They don't recognize him
in his abysmal condition. In keeping with good Jewish practice,
they sprinkle dust on their heads and sit on the ground with
him for seven days and seven nights. These acts of sympathy go
far beyond the response most of us give to others' misfortunes.
Though we come later in the story to understand the ways these
comforters are misguided or fail to recognize the deeper questioning and struggle to which Job has been called, we should be
edified by their costly and urgent sympathy.

What catches my eye in this brief account of these "first
responders" is that no one speaks a word to Job. For seven days
they simply sit with him. They don't abandon or ignore him, but
they understand that what the moment calls for is silent witness
— what many of us call a "ministry of presence." There is, as
the writer of Ecclesiastes might remind us, a time for speaking
and a time to remain silent. Knowing which is which is a matter,
every time, for careful discernment.

A few years ago when several of us were taking turns at the

bedside of a family member who was dying in a hospice house, I was surprised to be approached by a lovely, quiet woman — a stranger — who asked if she might be allowed to sit with her when we needed to be away for meals or other tasks. "I volunteer here," she explained. "I have felt a particular calling to be present to the dying. I don't speak; I just try to be present to them as I stay in my own place of prayer or meditation. I feel it's something I can offer, if you're willing." It was an unusual offer, but we accepted gratefully. Gently, without intrusion or further conversation, she slipped into the room when we were preparing to leave it and settled herself quietly into a chair by the bed, her hands open on her lap in a gesture of receptive prayer. In a sad and stressful season, that woman's gift of silence was powerful and memorable.

Her understanding of ministry was not unlike that of a pastor we know who goes to sites of public trauma — Rwanda, Uganda, Bosnia, Haiti, Northern Ireland — to "come alongside" those who are suffering and their caregivers. He goes as a pastor and a professional trained in treating post-traumatic stress disorder, but he is very clear that the first order of business for him is to listen and learn, and to be an open, available presence. Discerning the real needs rather than assuming he knows what they are requires real humility of one so well-equipped to wield professional skills and techniques, and teach them. The treating and teaching happen in due time, but they happen in the wake of a silence in which permission, trust, and readiness can emerge.

Job's comforters are good examples of kindness gone awry, but their first impulse offers us a striking reminder of what remains needful in times of great sorrow and suffering — to enter into the sorrow with compassion, imagination, and empathy, not hurrying to fill silence with words, but bringing a quiet presence and open hearts to places of pain that, being our brother's or sister's, are also our own.

But when you give a feast, invite the poor,
the crippled, the lame, the blind,
and you will be blessed, because they cannot repay you.
LUKE 14:13-14

It is not new news to readers of the Good News that there is blessing in caring for the poor, though we all need reminders to take that mandate personally, seriously, and radically into account as we move among the anonymous poor and disabled we pass daily in the streets of most cities. What takes me by surprise in the logic of Jesus' words here is the "because" clause. "You will be blessed," he promises, "*because* they cannot repay you." The idea is echoed in Jesus' rhetorical question: "If you love those who love you, what benefit is that to you? Even sinners love those who love them." Viewed from a certain angle, this appears to be one of those "harsh sayings" that seem not to compute with the air-brushed portrait of Jesus we're tempted to hang in our fearful hearts. We'd like a little credit for being loving people. For our thoughtful gifts to family, the casseroles we take to homebound neighbors, the volunteering we do among those who celebrate us at annual banquets.

The challenge of Jesus' promise of blessing in Luke 14 is at least twofold: first, try loving those who aren't inclined to thank you — who may even hold your efforts in contempt, because they live with the frustration and humiliation of having to be receivers with nothing to give; and second, try loving those who have no idea who you are — anonymously, foreclosing any temptation to seek recognition in your offering of time, money, or boxes of food. Those in the first category "cannot repay" not only because they lack material resources — so often through no fault of their own but because of systemic injustices in which we all participate — but also because they may lack a real motive to forgive you your part in that participation. Systemic poverty is too unfair, it's too long-term, and for many there seems no evidence of real political will among the privileged classes to share more equitably. "It is only your great charity," St. Vincent de Paul surprisingly wrote, "that will enable the poor to forgive you the bread you are able to offer them." Why should we be the ones who can enjoy being bountiful, generous, even lavish? The privilege from which our generosity comes is a blessing only if it fuels sustained, whole-hearted, empathetic action.

Those in the second category are the many to whom our money goes when we donate to organizations online, when we put checks in the Sunday collection plate for mission endeavors, when we perhaps leave something lovely on a doorstep or a desk where we know someone is suffering and needs encouragement. "Let not your left hand know what your right hand is doing" is another strong reminder of the intimate temptation to self-congratulation that requires intention and discipline to resist.

Every spiritual tradition teaches some version of "act without calculation," or "act in love and trust and leave the results to God," because, as T. S. Eliot put it, "For us, there is only the trying. The rest is not our business." Seeking thanks diverts us from being about our Father's business, which is always learning to walk a way of selfless love, caring about and for the poor, knowing we are in the same position they are — recipients of a divine generosity that we cannot possibly repay.

> ... and what does the LORD require of you but to do justice,
> and *to love kindness*, and to walk humbly with your God?
> MICAH 6:8

More than four decades after the fact, I remember the kindness of a teacher who saw that I was troubled and took his lunch hour to find out what was wrong and give me words of timely encouragement. I remember the way a woman who didn't know me at all welcomed me into her home as though she'd been waiting and hoping I, in particular, would show up at her door. I remember with great gratitude the words of a man who came to my mother's funeral to tell a story about the way her kindness to him changed his life. Acts of kindness do change lives in ways that go largely unmeasured.

The word "kindness," related to "kin," descends directly from the Old English *gecynde*, meaning "with the feeling of relatives for each other." Kindness extends our impulse to share with and care for others beyond the claims of the family we recognize as kin to those who have only the claim on us of their fellow humanity and their need. Kindness takes seriously that the children of God are in very fact brothers and sisters.

The Hebrew word that is generally translated as "kindness" is *chesed*, whose meanings range from "God's favor toward humankind" to "mercy toward the lowly and needy" to "instruction" (a shade of meaning in which teachers might take particular pleasure!).

There are several ways to "love kindness." One is to love being kind: kindness is a habit of the heart that keeps it open, welcoming, and hospitable and is, like a shared meal, its own reward. One translator points out a dimension of the word as it occurs in several of the psalms that sees kindness as a "quickening of spiritual life." Another way to love kindness is to appreciate others' kindness, recognizing and celebrating the acts of thoughtful generosity, attentiveness, noticing, and accommodating that weave community together. Far from the jealousy that fuels competition among those who do good "to be seen of men," witnessing another's act of kindness can allow us, if we are aligned with God's purposes for our life together, to rejoice in it for its own sake. Loving others' kindness deepens the mutual love that binds us together.

Hamlet's famous words to his mother, "I must be cruel to be kind," suggest a relationship between kindness and truth-telling.

Though scholars dispute his motives, it is clear that in the moment his urgent intent is to rescue his mother from a poisonous relationship with the man who killed her husband and usurped his throne. Though it bespeaks tenderness and softness of heart, kindness has its own vigor and clarity of purpose, and an edge that can be sharp.

Naomi Shihab Nye's poem "Kindness" brings out another dark dimension of that quiet virtue. "Before you know kindness as the deepest thing inside," she writes, "you must know sorrow as the other deepest thing./You must wake up with sorrow./You must speak to it till your voice/catches the thread of all sorrows/and you see the size of the cloth." She imagines the losses that erode plans and hopes, the loneliness of the anonymous passenger on the bus, passing by the scene of a death in the road and realizing it could have been you. These are ways of bringing us to identify with all human sorrows, to see our own mirrored in theirs. When we have tasted that salt from the great sea of sorrow, we may be made more aware and responsive to it in others. Then, as she writes in the concluding stanza, "it is only kindness that makes sense anymore." That we are walking the vale of tears with one another, that we will all have our turn for the losses and aches that can be assuaged only by tenderness, is an awareness that fosters the habit of kindness, imbedded as it is in Micah's ringing question between its companion virtues, justice and humility — the courage to care for others' rights and protection, and the awareness of who God is that makes humility not only a matter of rightly reckoning our dependence, but a matter for thanksgiving on our behalf and on others' for the care of such a Creator.

Whatever your hand finds to do, do it with your might. . . .

ECCLESIASTES 9:10

This simple directive has often brought me help in times of ambivalence. I'm endlessly capable of considering what lies "on the
other hand," so that often, while one hand is finding something
to do, the other hand is finding something else that looks equally
appealing. When Kierkegaard said "Purity of heart is to will one
thing," I believe he meant something like this: that when we bring
our energies fully into the present, and focus them fully on the
call of the moment, noticing what lies in front of us — assigned
or assumed or accidental — we align ourselves with the divine
power that is always available to us. We become channels of grace.
We enter into the kind of prayer Wendell Berry referred to when
he said, "Work done faithfully and well is prayer."

Studies have shown that the multitasking we've become so
accustomed to, if not indeed proud of, as we hold a steering
wheel in one hand, a sandwich in the other, and speak into a
hands-free device while we look for a parking place (I've done
this — I'm not proud of it) erodes our mental acuity. Far from
making our brains more agile, it seems to make them more
addled. It appears (I have this on good medical authority) that
multitasking, even if we do it "well," keeps us from entering
into the deeper parts of the brain where contemplation, reflection, and meditation take place. We find it harder to go to that

quiet place in ourselves where we hear our own most authentic voice — and God's.

It's not my point to inveigh against hand-held devices and video games . . . exactly . . . though I could, on slight provocation. My point here is to reflect on the promise of wholeness, mental and spiritual health, and deep alignment with God's purposes that can come of doing what we do with our whole might, and with our whole heart. Even in those instances where the "pros" and "cons" lists are about the same length, once we've made a decision — to sell the car or not, to accept the job offer in a new place or not, to head a committee or not — the time comes to let go of "the other hand," and do what our one open hand has found to do with all the energy that prayer, intelligence, and the help of those we trust can muster.

The story about Lot's wife turning to salt seems pertinent here, harsh though it is. For her, the consequences of looking back once the course is set are dire. Even when, for us, they are not dire or even dramatic, they are costly. Lingering ambivalence, working with a divided mind, wondering whether one should, after all, have chosen the other path, squanders the energy we need for the task at hand. Jesus said, "Let your yes be yes, and your no be no," encouraging his hearers to speak truth simply, and to make decisions cleanly, laying aside appealing alternatives for the sake of a wholehearted yes. The same advice may apply in this context as well: to say a clear and generous yes and move unimpeded in the direction of that assent is to step out on trust. Even if later we have to correct our course in some way, there is value in the act of trust itself, and the prayer that God may guide us through our uncertainties, letting us "learn by going where we have to go." The extent of what we learn will be commensurate with the "might" we invest in the going.

But *exhort one another* every day, as long as it is called "today,"
that none of you may be hardened by the deceitfulness of sin.
HEBREWS 3:13

Pastors get a lot of free advice from the people in the pews. It comes with the job: you're their pastor, and those who take that possessive pronoun literally often assume the task of training up their pastor in the way he or she should go. One of the more interesting pieces of advice my husband, a pastor, received early in his preaching career was "Tell us what to do!" His sermons at the time leaned toward exegesis: he liked to open up a text, consider the Greek or Hebrew meanings that add dimension to our understanding of the English words, show how the passage came out of a particular context, see how it invited us to reflect or pray or reconsider. He didn't tend to tell people what to do. But that parishioner was quite clear that what he hoped for and needed from a sermon was exhortation. He needed to go home with a renewed sense of direction and a little instruction on how to change his life and re-orient it toward Christ. (I've now taken it on as my occasional task, as he tinkers with his sermons on Saturday afternoons, to remind him, "Tell them what to do!")

Paul had no problem with exhortation. His letters are full of instruction about how to be the church: how to maintain proper conduct, how to care for each other's and the poor's physical and spiritual needs, how to resolve conflict. He told the people what to do. They saved those letters for good reason. Because of them we have his vigorous, much-disputed instructions to wrestle with as we work out our salvation in a very different world. More than a few contemporary readers I've talked with find Paul's insistent "do what I say" approach to leadership arrogant or irritating. I'm pretty sure he wouldn't have minded that; his radical commitment to the task of sharing the good news, and to the rich and challenging character of that good news, and to the One whose story he told gave him the conviction of the prophets whose "Woe unto you" messages weren't very popular, either.

Exhortation is more than instruction. The root word means "to incite," which goes beyond inviting or suggesting: when people are incited to action, it is as though someone has lit a fire under them. They can't stay still. They won't be silent. The urgency of political activists driven by a longing to heal a dying planet or by hearts that ache for the poor and long for just policies or by the horror of human trafficking or torture leads to a good deal of exhortation. We need that. We need it from the pulpits. And we need it from each other.

Even if we are properly charged and challenged and equipped and sent out by the leaders we trust, we can't afford to forget the immediacy and intimacy of this particular exhortation by the writers of Hebrews (some believe they were women): "Exhort one another every day." This means you and me — the laity. It means make a habit of it — not indiscriminate advice-giving, but mutual spiritual direction, deep honesty, and loving observation between those who are committed to helping one another "walk in love." It takes courage to do this. Most of us, at least in mainstream North American culture, are well trained to "mind our own business," and operate under a fairly narrow, individualistic notion of how far our "own business" extends. Should we stop someone from swatting a child? Being pushy? Gossiping? Spreading what we know are lies? Supporting policies we've studied and believe to be harmful to the poor?

It's good to ask ourselves when we witness another's troubling behavior whether we are the ones appointed by circumstance or role to address it, and whether the moment has come to do so. But those test questions need not become an excuse for avoiding the demanding and delicate task of loving exhortation. A church that can foster a climate of mutual trust and deep mutual obligation is a healthy church. It is one where members, because they do regard one another as family, know how to call one another gently and clearly to account. And "one another" is a key term. If your business is my business, mine is also yours, and we both recognize that careful, timely, loving correction is one of many forms of caregiving that sustain us as we find our way together through the dark wood and the vale of tears and stop by still waters and scale the mountain. If we're "in it together" in any meaningful sense, we can't afford the kind of niceness that avoids confrontation at all costs. We need to learn how to care for one another as animals groom one another — lovingly, playfully, intimately, sometimes insistently. They know they need one another to stay clean and healthy. So do we.

But Jesus *made no further answer,* so that Pilate was amazed.

MARK 15:5

One of the hardest moments to fathom in the story of Jesus' trial and crucifixion is this one, where he first answers his judges cryptically on the matter of whether he is, in fact, "king of the Jews": "You have said it." Then, leaving that provocative ambiguity hanging in the bristling air, he makes "no further answer." It is possibly the most consequential silence in history.

Why he refused to defend himself, especially when Pilate was evidently looking for an excuse to let him go, is a question that leads to much theologizing about the nature of his participation in the divine plan that led him to the cross. But what strikes me on a more personal level is the example he set in that moment of consummate restraint. Refusing to defend himself, he did, clearly, play into the hands of his executioners. But in that silence he also chose a way of wisdom I've remembered many times, usually belatedly, when my impulse has been to leap to my own defense.

I hate being misunderstood. I like approval. For those reasons I'm often inclined to explain myself if I think there's any danger of misunderstanding or disapproval. I imagine I'm not alone in that inclination. Years ago I was startled into examining that habit of self-defense, however, when I asked a friend, who seemed remarkably free of the need to explain herself, and at peace with her own decisions despite others' opinions, how she managed to avoid the temptation to defend herself when (as had happened several times) people passed judgment on her for the wrong reasons. Her answer was simple and rich with paradox: "I've found that it's liberating not to defend myself." The compulsion to self-defense, she was suggesting, is a trap. If we put our energies into assuring that no one will take our words the wrong way, object to our decisions, criticize our politics, impugn our motives, or pass judgment on our choices, we will use up a lot of the energy that could be available for more purposeful work.

Certainly clarity of intention and transparency about our motives are good, insofar as we can achieve them. Utter indifference to others' involvement in our lives and choices is no virtue. Still, having considered and prayed and shared our processes with those who have a right to know, and then having taken action, the call of the moment changes: the time for negotiation has passed, and our task is to put our whole hearts and our "whole might" into what we have decided to do, trusting that if we have chosen wrongly, the Holy Spirit will help with course correction.

"Don't complain, don't explain," my brother once said, sharing a simple credo that has served him well. Do what is given to you to do, faithfully, with sustained focus, taking the tradeoffs. "Just do it" can be a glib and simplistic way of avoiding the complexities of any process, but there is also something refreshing about that simple admonition. Do the thing given to you to do. Let your yes be yes. When your hand is on the plough, don't look back. Listen to those you trust, listen to and for the voice of God, and then let others' judgments blow past you like chaff. When the call is clear, the course will be clear. Silence may open the space you need then to step into with a wholeness of intention that shapes a channel through which courage can flow.

And *some fell into good soil and grew and yielded* a hundredfold.

LUKE 8:8

In an age of global crises — resource wars, climate change, and economic meltdown, to name a few — some argue that the most urgent crisis is soil depletion. Human life on the planet depends on the health of the few inches of topsoil under our feet. We haven't stewarded it very well. According to recent statistics, the United States is losing topsoil ten times faster (and China and India thirty to forty times faster) than the natural replenishment rate.

William Bryant Logan's remarkable book unremarkably entitled *Dirt* offers a long, reverent reflection on the life of soil. "How can I stand on the ground every day and not feel its power?" he asks. "How can I live my life stepping on this stuff and not wonder at it?" He connects the story of Moses' miraculous encounter with God to our own daily encounters with a source of energy no less divine or amazing: "All that is living burns. This is the fundamental fact of nature. And Moses saw it with his two eyes, directly. . . . God tells Moses, 'Take off your shoes, because the ground where you are standing is holy ground.' He is asking Moses to experience in his own body what the burning bush experiences: a living connection between heaven and earth. . . ."

We can't really separate care of the earth we were given from care of our own bodies, a duty that is, in turn, inseparable from care of our spiritual lives. So many of Jesus' parables and teachings depend upon the wisdom of good agriculture not only because he was speaking to people who tilled fields and tended sheep, but also because biology and ecology are sources of divine wisdom. Healthy soil depends on diversity of plant and insect life forms, on time to lie fallow, on careful plowing practices that prevent erosion by wind and water, on understanding root systems and sun and seasons.

At the level of individual action, this common wisdom seems to me to translate easily into the truth that gardening, yard care, water conservation, and pruning are, in fact — not only at the level of metaphor — spiritual practices. Caring for our creek-side backyard as well as voting for policies that may stop exploitive and unsustainable agricultural practices by industrial giants are ways of responding to Jesus' invitation to notice what good soil fosters. Indeed, we are the soil. We are the handful of dust a chemistry professor once brought to chapel: a handful of half a dozen elements, animated by the breath of the Spirit who breathes over the waters.

I read that the Hmong immigrants who live in California's central valley, many of whom are apartment dwellers with no land of their own, plant wherever they find a square foot of soil: in window boxes, between the sidewalk and the street, in small strips of flowerbeds others might disregard as inconsequential margins. Their humble recognition of possibility in small spaces helps me take new stock of what may be called abundance. San

Francisco has recently made efforts to support and subsidize rooftop gardening, allowing many city dwellers to reconnect their lives with what T. S. Eliot called "the life of significant soil." The significance of the soil can hardly be overestimated. We return to it in funeral services and on Ash Wednesday when we hear these familiar words: "Dust thou art, and to dust thou shalt return." Perhaps we need to hear those words more often, and to cultivate ways of caring more deeply and remaining more conscious of what it may mean to prepare the ground around us and within us to make them places where seeds may flourish.

These are the appointed feasts of the LORD, the *holy convocations,* which you shall proclaim at the time appointed for them.

LEVITICUS 23:4

Sunday mornings, when I was a child, we had pancakes and went to church. That's the way it was. We got dressed up in clothes we weren't allowed to wear the rest of the week since we were "saving" them for Sunday best. We gathered in a small church with men and women who were a little like extended family. I learned to sing harmony by following my mother's finger as it moved across the hymnbook and listening to her voice. We went forward for the "children's sermon" and colored in the margins of bulletins while we listened to the longer one for grown-ups. We did these things as a matter of course. They were a weekly routine — valuable, but unsurprising. It has only been in retrospect that I have come to recognize those weekly gatherings as "holy convocations."

Since ours was a "low-church" tradition, we maintained only a vestigial notion of the liturgical year, mostly a marking of Christmas and Easter, the rest being studies of particular books of the Bible, sermon series on the parables, and occasionally an excursus through parts of the Old Testament. Still, we came together in our understated way to commemorate, to celebrate, to reflect, to pray, and to attend to God and each other in what was mostly ordinary time spent among ordinary people who could see beyond each other's ordinariness in their weekly witness to God's grace and the goodness of fellowship. We believed ourselves quite literally to be called together for a holy purpose; the word "Sabbath," though it had also been through generations of American adulteration, still meant "something set apart." My mother tried not to shop on Sundays except when emergency hospitality demanded it. We put the white tablecloth on the dining room table and took our time over the noon meal. When money was scarce, as it often was, it was the one time in the week when we had pot roast or chicken, delicacies that were served on our grandmother's best china. Not infrequently there were guests, invited home after church and entertained with a mix of family lore and opinions of the day's sermon.

These, too, were holy convocations. We were called together by God for God's own purposes, and we learned that our gathering was an act of rightful and joyful obedience. We were called together because Christian life was not first of all about individual spirituality but about learning to be members of one body who were incomplete without one another. We were called to come into his presence with singing, into his courts with praise, and into each other's lives and stories with compassion and casseroles.

When we gathered, it was always a little disorderly and messy — as human gatherings always are. Someone (often my mother, a "deaconess" for decades) had to wash the little communion cups and iron the white linen altar cloth. Someone had to spirit away the restless seven-year-olds and rock the crying babies when the pastoral prayer exceeded a seemly length. Someone had to count the offering money and take it to the bank, and dust the pews, and repair the leaking pipes in the church basement. Sometimes the pastor had a cold. Sometimes the choir sang off-key. But we also learned this — that the call to be perfect as our Father in heaven is perfect was not a call to perfectionism, but an invitation to let ourselves be completed, permeated through and through with the breath of the Spirit that sometimes escaped in shared laughter and sometimes in halting words. In the short story "Fidelity," Wendell Berry writes of a family gathered around the bed of a dying man. Berry speaks of their belonging not to the world of professional hospital care, but to the "larger, looser, darker order of their merely human love." Those are holy orders — those variegated gatherings of relatives and church folk — and wherever two or three of them gather in love, it is a "holy convocation."

. . . from heaven the L ORD *looked at the earth,*
to hear the groans of the prisoners. . . .

PSALM 102:19-20

"Who ain't a slave, tell me that," Ishmael asks in the opening
chapter of *Moby-Dick* — a highly fraught question in 1851 America, divided as the country was between slaves, slave owners, ab-
stainers, and abolitionists. In an age when one in five African-
American men in the U.S. will go to prison, and when over seven
million adults are incarcerated and over three thousand on death
row, and when so many outside prison are entangled in crippling
debt, bankruptcy, and soul-numbing minimum-wage jobs, we
might well revisit that question: "Who ain't a prisoner?"

Some years ago, two of my students got into a heated debate about whether state health care for prisoners was adequate.
One of them, after presenting what he thought were compelling
financial statistics, capped his argument by observing, "We're
talking about criminals, anyway. Why should we provide them
with health care?" It was a thoughtless comment from someone
too inexperienced and fresh from high school to be held fully
accountable for such callous dismissiveness. Still, it was my job
in that moment to challenge both his categories and his ethical
reasoning. It seemed to come as news to him that not all prisoners
are criminals — that in fact between 2.5 and 5 percent of prisoners, by numerous judicial estimates, are innocent of the crimes

for which they're incarcerated, which means tens of thousands of innocent people behind bars in this country. This, of course, is not to mention the number of the "guilty" whose actions were born of desperation and poverty, and deserve mercy, or the certifiable criminals, many of them with white collars, who drive around freely in their BMWs. Compassion might be extended to prisoners for that reason, if for no other.

But there are others. Because those in prison have often been victims of violence before they were perpetrators. Many are there whose nonviolent crimes began in hunger or in life-threatening peer pressure or in lives begun and condemned to poverty and powerlessness. Even the most violent, though they need to be in custody for our sakes and theirs, are fearfully and wonderfully made — beings like us, knit in their mothers' wombs and called to repentance by an infinitely merciful God. They make visible the consequences of social, economic, psychological, and spiritual forces that deliver the wages of sin to a fallen world. But each one of us has our own imprisoning addictions or attitudes or guilt or envy or fear. And the message of the psalmist is that God hears the groans of prisoners — those behind bars and those who roam free. God visits us in our imprisonment, reminding us that there is freedom to be had and a justice system that exceeds all our wildest hopes for a merciful reckoning.

"I was sick and in prison and you visited me," Jesus says, teaching the disciples about the criteria God will apply on the Day of Judgment. Coupling the two states — sick and in prison — he invites us to see them as comparable. Both are states of constriction and suffering. Both are manifestations of our utter

dependence and brokenness. Both lead us in our pain to cry out
— for relief, for justice, for mercy, for comfort, for the love that is
always available from the One who hears our groans and answers
us, meeting us even "in the depths of Sheol."

. . . so that you may not be sluggish, but *imitators*
of those who through faith and patience inherit the promises.
HEBREWS 6:12

When our children were young, we entertained ourselves occasionally with an imitation game. "Do a Mommy gesture," I'd
challenge one of them. "Do a Daddy gesture." And they would
imitate us with amusing and unsettling accuracy. That our children learn by imitating us is a fact that should keep us humble
and watchful of what we teach them — and properly penitent
for what we've done and left undone in their vigilant presence.

Protestants have generally curtailed the Catholic practice of
holding up named and recognized saints for recognition, venera-
tion, and imitation. But here in Hebrews we are clearly enjoined
to pay attention to those whose lives offer us images of courage,
obedience, faithfulness, kindness, humility, and, of course, love
in its many-splendored variety. In fact, imitation is held up as
the opposite of sluggishness: it requires close attention, moving
outward from one's unthinking habits into patterns of being and
behavior that can, if we imitate well, reshape us.

The walls of the Cathedral of Our Lady of the Angels in Los Angeles are lined with images of saints whose lives map centuries of Christian history. All their faces are oriented toward the altar; they stand around and with the worshippers who occupy the pews between them. In St. Gregory of Nyssa Episcopal Church in San Francisco, the rotunda that houses the communion table is similarly alive with fanciful portraits of saints (very broadly defined in that community) who encircle those who gather at the table. *Here we are,* they seem to say. *Remember our stories. They will help you. We will help you. We're in it together.*

One of the best tools, I have found in years of teaching writing courses, is close and careful (even slavish!) imitation of good writers. Find a passage you love by Thoreau or Henry James or Hemingway or Annie Dillard, a stanza you love by Mary Oliver or Gerard Manley Hopkins or Rabindranath Tagore, or a haiku by Basho, and imitate it as closely as you can — its rhythm, its syntax, its patterns of repeated sound, its structure, its use of image or metaphor, of allusion, of punctuation. Do a Wendell Berry sentence. It's a little like "doing a Daddy gesture." You observe in order to imitate in order to acquire a skill, but more than that — in order to try out a way of thinking, saying, seeing, and situating yourself that will enhance and complicate your life, the way a new chip in a kaleidoscope complicates the pattern.

"Sing to the Lord a new song" used to strike me as a curious commandment. What's the matter with the old songs? I wondered. What about the affirmation of tradition in ancient words and rituals? But reflecting on the call to imitate the saints suggests one way of hearing that summoning to newness: climb out of the grooves you have dug; look around and find someone who has something to teach you as you navigate your own path; learn what they have to teach — try it out, try it on. In borrowing others' points of view, we enrich and diversify our own, and equip ourselves for compassion in recognizing our neighbors as our teachers, as members of the Body of which we are also members and, in very truth, as ourselves.

> . . . but in the seventh year there shall be a Sabbath
> of *solemn rest* for the land, a Sabbath to the LORD.
>
> LEVITICUS 25:4

Solemn rest is to be taken seriously — not simply as a welcome respite from work, but as a task of its own kind, prepared for and carried out with ceremony and clarity of purpose. The solemn rest prescribed here is not just for those who work the land, but also, and more explicitly, for the land itself. The fields must lie fallow. The earth must be allowed to renew itself.

The principle of letting fields lie fallow is good agriculture, no longer practiced by the corporate farms that force-feed chemical fertilizers to exhausted soil to make it bring forth fruit far beyond its "due season." It is also a good spiritual practice, since it requires that the farmer relinquish productivity and profit in costly and right acknowledgment that we do not live by bread alone, and that the earth is the Lord's — not ours.

Solemn rest is also advice more honored in the breach than in practice among the very busy working folk I know who have mostly been acculturated (I might even say brainwashed) to make a virtue of incessant busyness. I include myself, alas, among this benighted number. I remember being awakened to the need for reassessment of all that "productivity" by a colleague who bravely inquired, at a meeting of faculty and administrators, "When are we going to stop rewarding each other for doing too much?" It was a challenging question. Really to recognize workaholism as the pathology it is (not to mention as a variety of the sin of presumption) requires a countercultural, critical distance on our entrenched habits that is hard to achieve. I'm still grateful to my gutsy colleague for that question. I hang onto it in pressured times.

In the work I now do with medical students and doctors — dedicated people who are committed in inspiring, authentic ways to healing the sick and bringing health care to the underserved — I am struck by how many of them, though they doubtless prescribe bed rest to many a patient, function on too little sleep and double shots of espresso. Nor is it likely that the patients they advise take enough rest unless they're driven to it by physical exhaustion or a body cast.

I wonder sometimes if we're afraid of rest. We're conditioned by 24/7 news and Facebook updates to be afraid we'll miss out on something we "ought" to know. We're afraid we'll lag further behind in the race to some steadily receding finish line like Archimedes' tortoise. We're afraid we'll let someone down, as others' expectations expand to fill the mental space we allot them. We're afraid we won't measure up to the frenetic standards of celebrated overachievers. We're afraid, perhaps, that what we've been avoiding thinking about will surface to haunt and trouble us if we quiet our spinning minds.

Rest requires trust. The spirituals that encourage us to lay our burdens down are repositories of deep wisdom that comes from overworked people — slaves — for whom rest was a gift to be cherished and a promise full of life-giving hope. There are those who are bound to work by grinding poverty or economic enslavement. For them, rest, like food, is a fruit of justice we should all be helping to seek. For the rest of us, who have a choice in the matter, restoring solemn rest may be more a matter of stopping, reassessing our overwrought work ethic, and learning from the "siesta cultures" that allow everyone a midday nap or the dwindling sects where Sabbath is formally observed. Or from people who "set a spell" on verandas and visit, or who gather to share food and music on Friday evening. Or from the quiet ones in monasteries and meditation centers who find rest in silence. They can help us remember what rest looks like, and reclaim it not only as a gift from a wise Creator, who designed us to need it, but as a sacred command with wide application: "Remember the Sabbath, to keep it holy."

Whatever you do, *work heartily,*
as for the Lord and not for men. . . .

COLOSSIANS 3:23

I suppose I first heard the word "hearty" applied to appetite — a vaguely approving adjective, at least when the appetite in question belonged to a growing male child. Since I was not a male child, it was a little less clear to me that a hearty appetite was a matter for general approbation. When I began reading Victorian novels, "hearty" appeared as a descriptor of certain character types, never those of delicate sensibilities, refined intellect, or class, but people (again, usually males) with rosy cheeks and big hearts who frequented pubs and bought drinks all around. Likeable. Cheering company. Hale fellows, well met.

A deeper meaning of "hearty" — full of heart, distinguished by a loving and generous disposition — dawned on me some time later. I began to think of "hearty" as opposed to "heady," the latter referring to those whose inclination to analyze the rational argument often overrode their spontaneous and unguarded felt responses, and subordinated empathy to ideas. In that sense, to do one's work "heartily," as Paul recommends, might mean to do it without self-serving calculation, thought of reward, or anxiety, but rather stepping into our assigned tasks with clarity of purpose, trust in the Spirit's direction, and even deep pleasure in accepting what is given us to do.

The admonition to work "heartily" suggests also that we root our efforts in the deepest part of the soul or self — the Greek word is *psyche* — drawing strength from that underground spring from which living water may be drawn, so that our efforts depend not upon the limited energies under our conscious control, but rather upon the divine provision that comes always like manna, sufficient for the day, incapable of being hoarded.

Certain images help bring into focus the kind of work that is sanctified by this quality of whole-heartedness: Vermeer's *Lacemaker*, for instance — a woman so closely attentive to her intricate task, she seems unaware of her own loveliness or of the light-filled room. The word that comes to mind when I look again at this much-loved painting is "innocence." She is innocent of all distractions. Or I think of the exuberance of Thoreau's lengthy observations of Walden Pond as he saw it through successive seasons, noticing the light on its surface, taking the measure of its depth, turning it to metaphor and then to parable, enduring others' judgments for the sake of the task he deemed sacred. I think of the immigrants who farm the fields next to California highways, stooped low to gather strawberries or cut broccoli, working in conditions most of us would find worse than dismaying, but preserving in their steady labor a certain unyielding faith in human industry and resilience even in a context of economic injustice that I find both humbling and disturbing. They do what they must with a visible energy I wonder if I could muster.

Sometimes our work, like theirs, is to endure, as well as to engage. To do either heartily requires willingness and trust, focus and consent, a laying aside of the devices and desires of one's own heart in order to find one's peace in a deeper place — in the heart of God.

And he entered the temple and began to drive out *those who sold and those who bought* in the temple, and he overturned the tables of the money-changers and the seats of those who sold pigeons.

MARK 11:15

Buying is never innocent. When I buy, I participate in a process for which I assume a share of ethical responsibility. When I buy clothing made in an Indonesian sweatshop where children work long hours in locked factories, I support those practices. When I buy a soft drink from a company that's ruining the land of small farmers in India by dumping chemical waste into local soil and streams, I am not innocent of that destruction. In this familiar story of Jesus' outrage, I'm struck by his even-handed treatment of "those who bought and those who sold." The money-changers are no more at fault, it seems, than those who submitted to their usurious practices. Even the poor who bought pigeons for offerings bought membership in a system that turned spiritual practices and sacred space into opportunities for profit.

The kind of capitalism that dominates world trade now — so-called "free market" capitalism — commodifies everything in sight: land, water, airways, airwaves, genetic material, words, images, events, even human suffering and sorrow. Susan Sontag's last book, *Regarding the Pain of Others,* reflects with arresting acuity on the effects of war photography on "consumers" who look at images of mangled bodies and weeping families in the streets of Baghdad or Kabul, allow themselves a brief reaction or recoil, and then turn the page. Even if the intent is to awaken our moral imaginations or empathy, she suggests, such efforts can backfire simply because of the ways that photographs become saleable products. When more and more can be bought, it is increasingly difficult to retain a sense of the sacred — that which cannot be bought or sold, but must be entered into. It requires taking off our shoes and loosening our grasp on our goods and at least momentarily forgetting that "time is money."

The story of buying and selling in the temple is about allowing sacred places and practices to become extensions of the marketplace. The very word "sacred" means "set apart" — a bit of etymology worth remembering when we set up church Web sites, choose technology for worship spaces, or even buy food in bulk for the coffee hour. Church Web sites reflect the latest marketing techniques, linking to social media, offering rapid-fire, high-resolution images of attractive youth and families worshipping in well-appointed venues, and a variety of "services designed for you." It may be that any of these techniques in themselves are effective for genuine outreach, and build a bridge to those who may be leery of church and church people. It may be that using the idiom of contemporary market culture is one way of becoming, as Paul puts it, "all things to all people, so that by all means I might save some" (1 Cor. 9:22). But perhaps especially if our inclination is to appropriate new technologies, advertising techniques, social media, and marketing techniques to advance the causes we care about as followers of Jesus, it is important to ask ourselves regularly and reflectively what needs to be set apart and seen in different terms. How is worship space different from the social hall? How is the hour of worship different from the billable hour? The ancient question posed at Passover by the youngest child is a precious bit of the legacy we inherit: "How is this night different from all other nights?" Remembering the Sabbath to keep it holy is not only a practice but a principle meant, I imagine, to be extended to all those times and spaces and practices that have to be preserved and protected from the impingement of an economy that tends to absorb everything in its path.

In San Francisco, groups gather once a month for the "Really Really Free Market," where goods and services, food and fellowship are exchanged with no exchange of money. It's a little messy, but a festive and hospitable challenge to the idea that all exchange is subject to the laws of commerce. Certainly we, who have received a legacy of grace, can afford to consider widely and generously how sharing without scorekeeping may help sustain a way of life that is "free indeed."

Therefore, as the Holy Spirit says, "Today, if you hear his voice, *do not harden your hearts* as in the rebellion. . . ."
HEBREWS 3:7-8

Hardening our hearts is an option. Sometimes it's a necessity. Most of us know how to do it, because we've done it. Maybe, in some instances, we've had to do it. Emergency medical technicians and first responders have to harden their hearts to the wrenching cries of those in pain when causing a bit more pain is the only way to get them to a place of safety. Abused women have to harden their hearts to the disturbingly convincing pleas of their abusers (often masking a threat of further abuse) to "forgive" repeated violations and give them one more chance. Parents have to harden their hearts to a child's heartfelt desires when a "yes" would do harm in ways the child can't possibly understand.

So when the Spirit enjoins God's people not to harden their hearts, it is a reminder that hardening the heart is an entirely possible, and even conditioned, response that has to be resisted. A "soft heart" is vulnerable, susceptible to others' needs and ready to direct energy, time, and attention in ways one has not anticipated. A soft heart responds; a hard heart controls.

It is hard to be soft-hearted. If we allow ourselves to be touched by every ragged street person, every photograph of a suffering child in Ethiopia or Bangladesh or Kabul, every urgent appeal to give money for earth care, we will very likely end our days in emotional exhaustion and financial confusion. The soft-heartedness to which the Spirit summons us is not indiscriminate: love is discerning as well as patient, kind, and long-suffering. It is discernment that enables us to know when it is God's voice we hear — whether an impulse to provide care or change the day's agenda to accommodate someone's need is in fact a divine summoning or a distraction from perhaps less appealing matters that are ours to attend to. "Is that you, Lord?" is a useful question when such impulses arise.

There are ways to get a reliable answer to that question. We'd

all like the flash of heavenly light or an angel extending a hand
of blessing, but most guidance is likely to come in subtler ways.
To receive guidance, we need to practice the presence of God,
meaning a daily habit of listening in quiet to "what comes up"
when we lay aside preoccupations and open ourselves in prayer
and meditation. God nudges us — at least in my experience — so
it seems a good idea to pay attention to what keeps coming up
in odd and conspicuous ways, as well as those "out of the blue"
requests or invitations or opportunities. God's ways are not only
mysterious but often unconventional and counterintuitive. Attention to my own feelings also goes on the checklist. In his lovely
little book titled *God Is More Present than You Think*, Robert Ochs,
S.J., shows how God leads us by the desires of our heart, giving us
those desires — not just fulfilling them, but shaping them. Our
feelings, attractions, repulsions, hesitations, enthusiasms, and cu-
riosities are all sources of information about "what God is up to"
(as a pastor friend likes to say — a phrase that implies a playful
side to God that I find helpful and appealing). Sometimes the
voice of God is still and small. Sometimes it comes in a mighty
wind, or in the kind of abrupt and unavoidable intrusion that
seems to rise like a detour sign on our path that reads "Do you
get it yet?" Our work is to listen for it. And then, when we hear
it, when the answer to "Is it you, Lord?" is clearly "Yes," to accept
that summons without hesitation or excuse, without evasion or
excessive inquiry, and without fear, because all of those, however
reasonable they may seem, work like plaque in the arteries to
harden hearts God needs to remain soft and pliable if they are
to be shaped for divine purposes.

The high mountains are *for the wild goats;*
the rocks are a refuge for the rock badgers.
PSALM 104:18

Naturalist Bill McKibben calls our attention to this verse from
one of the great psalms of praise, emphasizing that consequential
little preposition "for." The mountains are *for* the wild goats, and
the rocks *for* the rock badgers — not just, not even primarily, for
us. The fir trees are *for* the storks. All creatures have their rightful
share in the abundance of God's provision.

I am troubled at times by the way the idea of humans' "dominion" over the earth is misapplied to justify unsustainable use
of "resources." Even the term "resources" implies a view of the
earth and its intricate natural systems that suggests it's all for us
— supplies for our sojourn here, rather than home to creatures
who have their own proper claim to it. A right understanding
of what it means to be given "dominion" over the creatures of
the earth surely has to take fully into account their dignity, their
beauty, and what they need to be sustained appropriately in what
is also their home.

In one of his memorable sermons, theologian George
Hunsinger pointed out the deep reciprocity between husband
and wife implied in the much-abused passage from Ephesians
that says the husband shall be head of the wife. God's mandate
to humankind in Genesis to "take dominion" is subject to similar

abuse. Taking dominion implies not simply appropriation for human use, but, more broadly and generously, oversight, responsibility, stewardship, care, loving attention to the needs of our fellow creatures, who have their own purposes — who play and care for their young; who spread their branches under the sun, and, if they are oaks, share nutrients through interconnected root systems; who call to one another over miles of woodland and fly in formation without instruction; who gather in beautifully designed hives and make sweet honey; who migrate thousands of miles and sit patiently for weeks to keep small eggs warm.

One reason to take children to wild places, or even into the back garden where they can spot worms or pill bugs and listen for birds, is to cultivate a sympathetic interest in the lives of other creatures that won't go away later when incentives to destroy habitats and "develop" wild places present themselves as temptations. Already, species are disappearing at more than a thousand times the natural extinction rate. I don't want to imagine a world without birdsong or streams without the flash of trout scales. Who are we without them?

A world where everything is "for" us may seem like a gift of abundant provision, but every traditional culture in the world understands that gifts are for sharing, and that hoarding destroys the life and livelihood of the community. We need our fellow creatures not just because they provide us with food and fur, but because they are companions on this earth who have things to teach us, and whose value lies not just in their utility, but in the mystery and beauty of their aeronautically perfect wings or translucent fins or floppy ears. They have their burrows and eyries;

the mayfly and the tortoise have their life cycles, and teach us that some lives are short and some long. Some lives are intensely local and some are wandering. And the prey and the predator are one, in ways that challenge simplistic anthropomorphic moral categories. They are not us. They are not like us, in important ways. We need them and they need us while we find our respective and intersecting ways on the earth that is ours to share.

. . . worship the LORD *in the beauty of holiness.*
PSALM 29:2

I had the privilege once of serving on a committee charged with designing a new worship space — a task that opens rich reflection on what "sacred space" might mean. The psalmist longs to "gaze upon the beauty of the LORD and to seek him in his temple," to be kept "safe in his dwelling," and hidden "in the shelter of his tabernacle." And he longs for "the beauty of holiness."

The desire for safety and sanctuary is not entirely separable from the desire for beauty. The church is a dwelling place. It is, in a sense some of us have yet to experience most fully, our home. It is where we come into community with people we didn't choose, but who were, like us, chosen and adopted as the children of God. It's where we work out our differences and extend hospitality. The church is also a place where we are invited to gaze on the beauty of the Lord and to "worship . . . in the beauty of holiness." This last phrase is disputed by scholars and translators. Some believe it refers to God's own beauty and splendor. Others believe it refers to the beauty and splendor of the priestly garments that are to be worn in the house of God. What both translations suggest is that worship calls us to turn our attention to what is beautiful.

Paul instructed the Philippians, "Finally, brothers, whatever is true, whatever is honorable, whatever is just, whatever is pure, whatever is lovely, whatever is commendable — if there is any excellence, if there is anything worthy of praise, think about these things" (4:8). This is not an invitation to avoid the hard, dark, complicated business of working out our peace with each other in a world of violence and conflict, but to attend to what is true and beautiful even in the midst of violence and conflict.

The church is a place where we may encourage one another to do that — to lay down our newspapers and our flags for a while and remember that we are already citizens of the kingdom, that Christ, who is its head, has already accomplished victory over death and sin, and that he is altogether lovely. To make the physical setting of worship as beautiful as we can is to honor the Lord of all beauty in heaven and earth. The colors, textures, shapes, and sounds that please the eye and ear and delight the imagination are God's good gifts.

One of the most powerful testimonies I've ever seen to the human need for beauty was in the concentration camp at Dachau, where a display case held tin cups and plates that prisoners in that living hell had bothered to decorate, etching designs with nails to beautify them for use in secret acts of worship. Surely their humbling example is something to learn from: beauty matters, especially in worship — recognizing it, creating it, finding in it a kind of sanctuary from the world and its violence, a kind of comfort and assurance that what is "altogether lovely" has not perished from the earth, and that because that is true, all that is lovely is ours to celebrate and cherish.

I was sick and you visited me, I was *in prison and you came* to me.
MATTHEW 25:36

The horrifying realities of prison life, especially in places where suspected "terrorists" are held and subjected to deprivations, humiliations, and cruelty, came into sharp focus when I attended a conference called "Theology, International Law, and Torture." Among those who attended were survivors of torture, international lawyers, theologians, and representatives from a wide variety of human rights organizations and churches.

Torture is not something most of us want to hear about. The first speaker was Sister Dianna Ortiz, now Director of Torture Abolition and Survivors Coalition International, the only organization founded by torture survivors. Its mission is to abolish torture wherever it occurs. Sister Dianna, a missionary, was tortured in a Guatemalan prison where she was incarcerated on suspicion of helping local farmers with plans for insurrection. (She was, as many imprisoned in such situations are, innocent.) In the midst of almost unthinkable abuse, she promised God, herself, and fellow sufferers that if she survived and returned to the U.S., she would tell her story. She found, upon her return, that very few wanted to hear what she had to say. Church and state alike met her testimony with indifference, evasion, or denial. Her story was hard to hear even for those of us who had quite deliberately gathered to listen, seated on comfortable chairs there in a climate-controlled lecture room. But it is a story that deserves to be told, along with many others of the kinds of suffering taking place in prisons where those who suffer and those who inflict suffering are all being deeply damaged.

Sister Dianna's innocence, of course, lent particular poignancy to her story. In the course of her talk I remembered another I'd heard sometime previously by a lawyer from the Innocence Project, a nonprofit organization committed to reviewing the cases of people who may have been wrongly convicted. Hundreds who have spent time in prison, some on death row, have been proven innocent and been released as a result of this organization's work. It is, in some ways, a thankless task. The way of least resistance for any of us is to choose to believe that the justice system is just, that all who are in prison are "criminals," and that criminals deserve punishment. But all of those assumptions are flawed, and deserve re-examination each time we hear another story of crime and punishment.

Every generation has its own reckonings to make with abuses of power and gross violations of basic human rights. Many of us manage to postpone that reckoning by one of three common strategies: denial, legitimation, or personal exculpation. Relatively few churches are willing to speak out on the issues of prison conditions, routine abuse, and torture. Why, when the duty to attend to those in prison is so explicit? How are we carrying out the mandate "to care for the powerless, to do justice and love mercy"?

A question that kept coming back to me in the course of the conference on torture is this: What am I willing to know about? How do I protect myself from knowing what threatens my assumptions? Whether or not I drive across the bridge to visit inmates at the state penitentiary, they are my brothers and sisters, and the least I can do for them, I think with lingering discomfort, is be willing to hear the stories of hidden lives that so often entail abuses none of us should tolerate.

Since the conference on torture, I have listened to news reports about prisons with a little more attention. They are occasions to pray for inmates and wardens, for all who minister to them, and for all who participate in a justice system that is deeply infected by racism, greed, and indifference. They are also occasions to be grateful for nonprofits like the Innocence Project, or the Restorative Justice Project, or Planting Justice (a group that trains prisoners and hires them upon release to do garden work), or the Prisons Foundation, which publishes prisoners' writing and exhibits their art. If I can't go to the prisons myself (and the reasons I can't deserve to be reassessed periodically), I can support those who do, remembering in those efforts how little separates me from prisoners whose stories are never simply about criminality or evil intent, but about poverty, loss, illness, sorrow, vulnerability, broken systems, broken hearts. May my heart be broken by what breaks the heart of God.

Mystery and Surprise

In the fullness of time . . .
GALATIANS 4:4

TIME SWELLS, BREAKS, AND EBBS. One hour in a life can change the whole of it. In moments of significant decision, it has often seemed to me that the decision has already been made, and is only now, like the shoot of a young plant after a time of germination, emerging into visibility. I don't "make" the decision so much as recognize it.

And so, in the fullness of time, it comes to pass. It would be easy to be too glib about the idea that things happen when we are ready for them. But there is a sense in which, at least in retrospect, we may see how life has prepared us even for those things that take us completely — and not always pleasantly — by surprise.

We don't know, even now, what we are being prepared for — what seeds are breaking and sprouting in the fertile dark of the unconscious mind or in the body. When the idea that was only a wispy dream image becomes a thought, we may forget its mysterious beginning, and forget that it is gift as much as invention. When the cancer cell becomes a tumor, we may not stop to think that we have been carrying it for months, maybe years. But all of us do. The seeds of life and the seeds of death commingle like wheat and tares. In the fullness of time, when we finally see what has been with us all along, we may also see how we have been prepared, subtly and steadily, to meet it, rise to it, dive into it, learn from it.

In *This Cold Heaven,* her memoir about seasons spent in northern Greenland, Gretel Ehrlich wrote about the long winter, when darkness covers both day and night: "Darkness reconciles all time and disparity. It is a kind of rapture in which life is no longer lived brokenly." So much happens in the dark time of the year — germination, hibernation, bundling, burrowing — and those things that are covered over are protected for a time and allowed to mature. There is a wholeness in that deep, secret process, and in what gathers in us to lead us into the next season of our lives. We are being prepared for the suffering, the celebration, the loss, the discovery, the letting go that will be called for. Our work in those seasons of darkness and unknowing is not simply to wait, but to await, with trust and open intention, expecting that what will happen is already happening, and will come to pass in due time, and to give time its due. Then, when our days have reached their fullness, they will be poured out, rich and ripe, shimmering like grain in late summer light. And we will be surprised by what has come to pass in ways, and for reasons, we couldn't have fathomed before.

Praise him, you highest heavens. . . .
PSALM 148:3

NASA recently discovered a bubble of concentrated energy rising from the plane of the Milky Way galaxy that extends 125 million light years above and below it. On the digital photograph taken through the Fermi telescope and a later, clearer reconstructed image, it looks like the bioluminescent body of a jellyfish emerging, astrophysicists believe, from a black hole at the center of the galaxy. If, indeed, a vast body of energy has exploded (over the past four million years — not long by astro-historical standards) from within a black hole, those phenomena need further examination.

The scope, intensity, and duration of activity among the stars, planets, and galaxies are literally beyond human imagination. Those who study them find a way to get comfortable with numbers figured in powers of ten, distances that defy analogy, and mind-bending concepts like eleven dimensions and worm holes and string theory. But even they, as many in the field have acknowledged, are driven to awe.

The highest heavens are moving in their own courses, the universe expanding, stars exploding. And what has all of this to do with us small folk on earth? What does our praise have to do with all that astro-activity? Three things, at least. One is that the visible heavenly bodies give us daily evidence of divine order and power, magnitude and magnificence, stability and change. The sky offers its testimony to the Creator in ways we are perhaps too quick to call "inanimate."

A second way in which the heavens have to do with us and our praise is that they have given guidance to wise men in the desert and to sailors on the sea — helpful, predictable, practical navigational guidance. We have charted our courses by them and learned from them the patterns of the universe we inhabit. Our knowledge of the earth is not separable from our knowledge of the heavens, and the heavenly orders are literally part of Creation's song.

A third way in which the heavens join us in praise is in their light. The two great "God is" statements in Scripture are "God is love" and "God is light." Light, it appears, is more than metaphor. It is God's love and power made visible. Astronomers measure distance in light years — how far light travels in a year. Light is the primal energy sent forth on the first day of creation. By it we live and see and come to know who and where we are. When we are born, we open our eyes into it. Some who are congenitally blind have said they can sense it. When we die, so we learn from clinical death stories, we yearn toward a summoning light. The scattering of light we see in the stars is a nightly reminder of what the darkness has not yet overcome. "Praise him, you highest heavens" might well be understood as an affirmation of what the heavens in fact do. Proclaim light. Beautify the darkness. Let themselves be moved. Die when it is time, sending their last rays earthward as gift and guidance.

Do you know *when the mountain goats give birth?*

JOB 39:1

I have forgotten much of what I learned in biology courses, but I do remember a simple sentence from a remarkable lecture on the nature of scientific investigation: "Every mystery you uncover reveals another mystery." The whole litany of animal life in Job 39 is a long and humbling reminder of those mysteries. We know a great deal about the animal world at this point. No doubt some graduate student has spent lonely nights in a tent to find out when, in fact, mountain goats give birth. But even learned obstetricians who devote their lives to understanding human birth can only approximate due dates, and would be the first to admit how much of their expertise is guesswork. Germination is a secret that each woman, like each mountain goat, works out in complex, unconscious negotiation between her body, her child's body, and the environment she inhabits. Even the most informed among us don't know all there is to know about what we carry in the double helix that gives our minds and bodies their first and last instructions.

When the 2001 film *Winged Migration* first came out, it took me some time to decide to see it, since the friend who urged me to do so dryly described it as two wordless hours of watching birds fly. I like words. And I see birds fly every day. So I didn't hasten to the theater, but let the pressure build as others marveled over the beauty and power of the production. Finally I watched it. I was riveted and moved. The mystery of the inexplicable knowing that guides flocks thousands of miles in "due season" is, in the most precise sense, awesome. We can study their flight patterns, their schedules, their feeding, mating, and hatching habits, but we can't *know* them beyond the limits of our very human understanding, though we may broach that knowing as we consent to see them more in their terms, and less in ours, willing to imagine their needs, their purposes, their connection to the Spirit who, as Gerard Manley Hopkins beautifully put it, "over the bent world broods with warm breast and with ah! bright wings."

Annie Dillard, among other "pilgrims" in the natural world, approached its creatures with that kind of open heart and mind. She writes with remarkable spiritual insight about those encounters with other species that stun us into humility. In *Teaching a Stone to Talk,* she describes coming upon a weasel in the woods who met her gaze and held it: "Our look was as if two lovers, or deadly enemies, met unexpectedly on an overgrown path when each had been thinking of something else: a clearing blow to the gut. It was also a bright blow to the brain, or a sudden beating of brains. . . . The world dismantled and tumbled into that black hole of eyes." This lifting of the veil that separates species sounds very like C. S. Lewis's description of being "surprised by joy." We don't really know the weasel or the migrating bird or the mountain goat. But that there is something (or someone) there to know, fashioned by the same hand that gathered us from dust, is a mystery worth pondering regularly and humbly. As Emerson writes in a little poem addressed to a forest flower, "Why thou wert there, O rival of the rose,/I never thought to ask; I never knew;/but in my simple ignorance suppose/the selfsame power that brought me there, brought you."

. . . for I am fearfully and wonderfully made.
PSALM 139:14

Anyone who has studied anatomy has very likely come to moments of sheer amazement. That white cells rush to the scene of injury; that hormones carry intricate regulatory messages to every organ; that chemical signals passed between neurons allow us to react with lightning speed to pain or noise; that the liver protects us from all manner of toxins, enduring the insults of bad eating and drinking habits, sometimes for years. That all our interlocking systems function so well so much of the time despite junk food, inadequate exercise, and exhaust fumes is cause for wonder, indeed. Even illness gives cause for wonder, not just at the complexities of pathology, but at the body's many built-in resources for healing itself.

Mind studies are even more amazing. How people recover from strokes, what may survive the ravages of Alzheimer's, and what the brains of athletes, mathematicians, physicists, linguists, musicians, and artists can process as they grapple with the challenges of their fields bring us to the edge of wonder. The power of what we call "will" and "spirit" takes us beyond that edge.

We know from the examples of martyrs, saints, and heroes, as well as the courage and clarity of "ordinary" people who rise to extraordinary occasions, that we have it in us to lift the Volkswagen off the victim or face down the riot police. We barely know our own capacities.

Growing interest over the past decades in bringing Western and Eastern medical traditions into dialogue has opened up new avenues of reflection for all of us on the mind-body-spirit complex that we know as self. That "trinitarian" relationship, to borrow a term, is a mystery that Asian medicine has embraced more fully than technology-dominated American medicine, where marvelous feats of surgery can be performed, but where patient care and gentle reinforcement of the body's own healing processes sometimes dwindle in the harsh and glamorous light of all those dazzling technical successes.

As the nation continues to struggle with the problem of providing adequate health care, we might do well to consider how, within our faith communities, we might include reflection on the life of the body in our efforts to shore up the life of the spirit. Care of the sick is one of Jesus' clearest mandates, and reaches back far beyond him into ancient prescriptions for community life. We might ask ourselves what we can learn from the patterns of illness most prevalent among us — cancer, diabetes, obesity, behavioral disorders — about the condition of our common life. Or how illness and injury call us to attend to our own bodies and each other's.

Those bodies are not only wonderful, but fearful — a strange word in English, and not easy to engage. In Hebrew the word means, roughly, "with great reverence, heartfelt interest, and respect." We were made with divine intention, objects of divine interest, and even of God's own respect for creatures "a little lower than the angels" capable of coming into lively relationship with their Creator. We can certainly be fearsome: we can do each other great harm in our ambiguous ingenuity. We are also capable of exercising powers whose outer limits we've hardly explored; Olympic athletes, astronauts, and gifted healers offer only a few among many examples of the reach of our possibilities. Deep respect for our own capacities can and should drive us to deeper faith in the One who can bring those potentials to fruition, and to prayer for ever-deepening understanding of God's purposes in giving us life in these bodies on this planet at this time.

When one rules justly over men, ruling in the fear of God,
he *dawns on them like the morning light.* . . .

2 SAMUEL 23:3-4

There may be no more beautiful vision of what rightly exercised power looks like than this from Second Samuel. The light of dawn is silent and gradual. It spreads evenly across the landscape, making visible what has been shrouded in darkness. It enables one to distinguish one thing from another clearly, and to find one's way. It warms and heartens, but also exposes the night's secrets and drives predators into hiding. Colorful, sometimes, it also brings out the colors in all it touches, and, as it does so, becomes something to see by rather than something to see. What a rich vision of leadership we are given here — a standard to encourage in those we elect and a standard to set ourselves when we find ourselves in positions of power.

I remember a time when I was anxious about how to step into a new role that carried new authority. A wise older friend said, "Begin by being. Enter the room with your body relaxed and your heart open, find your own center, take a breath, and stand there a moment until you're sure of your own balance. Then begin the conversation. Whatever tensions arise then, they won't easily dislodge your inner plumb line." Another time she said, "Be before you do." To "dawn on" others honors that priority: the judge who judges well stops, takes a long look, and listens carefully before acting. The speaker who inspires opens silences and breathes into them. The politician who takes seriously the welfare of the people meets their gaze, stands exposed without grandstanding, and allows himself or herself to receive new wisdom and revise opinions as new information emerges in the circumstances of each demanding day. We serve others best when we drive our roots deeply into these truths that are true for each moment: God is present; guidance is available; we have what we need for what we are called to do.

In the Kabbalah we find this apparently whimsical instruction: "Imagine that you are light." To undertake that exercise of imagination, however, takes us beyond whimsy and allows us to broach the experience of power and confidence suggested in Samuel's image of dawn. If we are light-bearers, if, as geochemists tell us, we are literally made of stardust, if all our atoms are moving and neutrinos stream through us, if we are composed of matter that was and will be energy, then imagining that we are light is a surprisingly practical way of coming to terms with something literally and importantly true about ourselves. The kabbalistic instruction is a call to pay attention to how we use the energies that we *have* and *are* — to consider how we use our power. We have power. We are powerful beings; the feeling of powerlessness that all of us experience sometimes, and some of us often, is not the truth about us. Rather, we are creatures to whom the Creator has given generous access to divine power.

In *Pilgrim at Tinker Creek,* Annie Dillard writes, "All things live by an infinite power, and dance to a mighty tune." When we are blessed to find ourselves among those who realize this and live into that dance, they "dawn upon us like the morning light." And this might be a worthy prayer to carry through a day of encounters: May we walk among others basking in their light and blessing them with ours, bowing to the light source who inhabits and illumines us both.

Provide for me a man *who can play well* and bring him to me.
I SAMUEL 16:17

In the midst of his pain, Saul asks for music. His request is not for particular songs he loves or for a person who knows him and is likely to be most eager to do his bidding. It is for a man who can play well. He needs a musician he can trust to provide music that will heal. Someone into whose hands he can put himself. That trust is a key factor in David's calling. David's skill on the lyre and harp, and most likely his voice, are essential factors in his unfolding story. His music lays the foundation for his work in the world as leader of God's people. It brings him into the company of the king, and into the deep, formative friendship with Jonathan. It gives him opportunity to develop the legacy of the Psalms, which has been one of the richest treasures of Judeo-Christian tradition. It keeps his own heart open, and softens Saul's. It nourishes and matures his relationship with the God he loves.

I'm struck by how this simple request shows how God works with our gifts. He makes them available to us — by genetic code or circumstance or desire or opportunity — and they're ours to develop. We may think we're developing them for our own pleasure, but the fact is that they're also ours for purposes we don't know at the outset. When David sat in the fields on long afternoons playing his lyre while the sheep grazed, he had no idea that his music would open a wide and consequential door to his future. Being a man who could play well made him a ready instrument in the unfolding history of Israel.

Our gifts are ours to develop and use, but right stewardship of them means being ready to put them at God's disposal. If someone calls for a person who can play well, or speak well, or write well, or design well, or listen well, or teach well, or who can design good software, we may not determine whether we're the one God will choose for a particular mission, but we can be available. Our job is to do well what we do and be ready when the invitation comes. I, for one, would love to see more people "who can play" in political office, education, and church leadership!

It seems important that in David's story, music is the gift that serves God's purposes. They are, at one level, political purposes. David is being prepared to be king, not the choirmaster or chief musician. But how like the Spirit to work indirectly in just this way. How like the God who is "Master of Surprises" to find a "man who can play" to govern a wayward people, hungry for a leader who can sing a new song.

He *put a new song in my mouth.* . . .
PSALM 40:3

Everyone I know who does creative work — songwriting, poetry, musical composition, painting — knows that working creatively is largely a matter of receiving. A good phrase or line is "given." It comes up, comes in, comes about in the process of playing with possibilities. We recognize it when it "comes." We know we didn't "make it up," but caught it like a fly ball or a falling apple. We are thankful.

The Psalms are full of this awareness of the gift character of good work and even good prayer: "O LORD, open my lips," the psalmist writes. It is God who gives gifts to those we call "gifted," and enables them to use them. Jesus reminds the disciples of this as he sends them out to preach and teach: "Do not worry about what you will say in that hour. It will be given to you" (Luke 12:11). The promise comes with a requirement of trust. It's a hard requirement for those of us who tend to obsess, over-prepare, over-control, over-plan. In fulfilling our overwrought work ethics, we may in fact close off avenues of grace that come so often through the back door of the unconscious or through a digression or an interruption or in a hot bath or while stacking blocks with small children.

Our share in the work we call "creative" (which includes all work done with mindfulness and kindly intention) is to prepare for those surprises. We train, we try things out, we practice, we get through the dull parts — the five-finger exercises and what Anne Lamott unabashedly terms "shitty first drafts." But if we learn to work in a spirit of receptivity and trust, we enter our working hours in a spirit of expectation. We make room in the course of things to consider and consent to the second thought, the belated and alternative idea, the oddball image that seems to come out of left field.

Sometimes a work will take new shape or direction by means of something as fleeting as a daydream — a remembered scene from a book or a movie, the image of a bird on the balcony railing, or the sound of wind in a grove of trees. Henry James claimed that his copious novel *The Portrait of a Lady* began with such a "seed": he remembered seeing, through an open doorway, two figures at a long window — a man, seated, and a woman standing next to him. The image suggested a story, and the story became one of the great American novels.

James may not have considered the Holy Spirit the source of his inspiration, but many do. Many have the experience of a "new song" or a new line or a new idea for a composition emerging in periods of prayer or sacred reading or contemplation. Those who are trained to recognize and receive such surprises know what to do with them. First they say thank you. Then they develop them with all the tools they have at hand — a sense of plot, a sense of color, a feel for instrumentation or choral composition.

Even in the ordinary tasks of ordinary life, we may be surprised by gifts of grace if receptivity becomes a habit. A hundred times a day small surprises await those who notice. Small, heart-opening encounters, impulses of kindness, consoling words, and new possibilities come to those who ready themselves and wait expectantly for the "new song" God may give them to sing, even as God gives the reason for singing. As an old Quaker hymn describes the economy of gift and Giver, "Since Love is Lord of heaven and earth, how can I keep from singing?"

And God said, *"Let there be light,"* and there was light.

GENESIS 1:3

This simple utterance, ascribed to God at the very beginning of the long, unfolding story of creation and salvation, is one of the most thrilling in all of Scripture. In a recent "TED talk," an astrophysicist described the "Big Bang" as an explosion of energy that, unlike most explosions, seems to have gained energy — and momentum — as it expanded, rather than dispersing and diminishing it. It seems, in other words, to have been a self-renewing, self-replenishing cascade of energy into a universe that is still expanding. How like God, I thought as I listened. His description gave new meaning to the phrase "new every morning," and to Mary Oliver's simple, startling lines, "Every morning/the world/is created."

The word that always gives me pause in this exquisite sentence about the birth of the universe is "Let." The grammatical subjunctive (let it be so; that it may be so . . .) is the language of blessing: "May the Lord bless and keep you." And of curse: "Let thorns grow instead of wheat, and foul weeds instead of barley" (Job 31:40). It is also the language of lawmaking and command: ". . . let every daughter live" (Exod. 1:16). "Let us abandon this exacting of interest" (Neh. 5:10). And the language of permission: "It is the LORD. Let him do what seems good to him" (1 Sam. 3:18). And the language of gathering and praise: "Let the heavens be glad, and let the earth rejoice . . ." (1 Chron. 16:31). And the language of great prayers of petition: "Let me hear joy and gladness; let the bones that you have broken rejoice" (Ps. 51:8). "Let me dwell in your tent forever! Let me take refuge under the shelter of your wings" (Ps. 61:4).

The paradox built into this little word lies at the heart of a life of faith. It expresses both power and relinquishment; both authority and submission; both intention and accomplishment. The sacramental dimension of words becomes beautifully clear in this one, as, in certain contexts, it makes present what it invokes. Jane Kenyon's lovely poem "Let Evening Come," written toward the end of her life, enacts, line by line, a hard-won and complete acceptance of the letting go that comes as daylight fades, and as life draws to its close. The word "let," which is repeated twelve times in the course of its six short stanzas, enacts that letting go as, one by one, the implements of daytime work and the familiar images of daily life are released into darkening evening. The final stanza, it seems to me, is worth carrying in our hearts as we sit with the dying, or face the fact of our own final days: "Let it come, as it will, and don't/be afraid. God does not leave us/ comfortless, so let evening come."

"Let" is a deep and active "yes" to what is and what shall be — an imitation of Christ and an act of trust in the One who promises freedom and joy we can barely imagine if we open our clutching hands and utter this little word of relinquishment that is also consent to divine blessing.

And Jesus, *looking at him, loved him. . . .*
MARK 10:21

I am touched by this curious little pause in the story of the rich young ruler. After an account of the young man's earnest questioning and offering of his spiritual credentials, we read that Jesus looked at him, and, seeing him in a new way, "loved him." Before answering the young man's question, Jesus pauses, apparently to take a second, closer look, fully considering the young man's desire for righteousness, his spiritual hunger, and also, apparently, his immaturity. Because it is a familiar story, we know that the young man fails the test Jesus must have known he would fail: the challenge to sell all he has, give to the poor, and become Jesus' follower.

Since I haven't given up my possessions, and know few who have, I realize most of us have no stones to throw at the poor, conflicted young man when he "went away sorrowing" because he couldn't bring himself to give up his wealth. I'm happy to pledge at church and contribute to the food bank, but I'll probably go to my grave clutching my laptop. Still, I don't think the point of the story is to invite our judgment of him, or of ourselves, for that matter, but to recognize how Jesus loves even those who aren't yet wholehearted, generous, or pure. He sees us with a deep, sustained, compassionate gaze. He turns toward us as toward the rich young man, listening to our imperfect prayers, to petitions that smack of self-righteousness and self-interest, seeing us through our learning moments, our resistances, and our spiritual failures.

In a certain way, this story complements the stories about the calling of the disciples. One by one, Jesus calls the Twelve to leave their nets, their careers, their families, their security and follow him — and they go. But many others who also follow him through the streets and into the temple go home after a public healing or a hillside sermon to continue plowing their fields, supervising their servants, preparing meals, raising children. They go away to continue pondering what it might mean to live in grace and reckon righteousness by love. They probably go home "sorrowing," or at least a bit envious of the few who seem free enough or sure enough or strong enough to follow Jesus along roads that lead away from everything they hold dear. I've certainly cast wistful glances at missionaries and Peace Corps volunteers and medical teams who pack up after their fund-raising events and head out for purposeful adventures in places where needs are unambiguous and a sense of useful accomplishment is virtually guaranteed.

The rich young man's story is about a kind of calling that is less miraculous, less dramatic, and more gradual than those of the twelve apostles. I don't think that disappointed applicant for the kingdom left without hope. I don't imagine Jesus' look of love was lost on him. I don't imagine he concluded, as he wound his way home, "Well, forget it, then. I guess godly life is not an option." I imagine he went home to a restless night and many days more of wrestling with what the Lord required of him — what it might really mean to love justice, do mercy, and walk humbly with God. And I imagine Jesus' love stayed with him, even haunted him, in the course of that painful growth process. He had a lot to sort out. I imagine that what might have sustained him as he groped his way to a new relationship with God was a look of complete, unstinting, divine love.

Truly, truly, I say to you, unless one is *born of water and the Spirit,* he cannot enter the kingdom of God.

JOHN 3:5

Jesus' explanations are often more confusing than clarifying. They challenge his hearers to make a quantum leap to a new level of understanding — symbolic, spiritual, even mystical. This line from John 3 is his answer to a question that seems either silly or sarcastic: "Can [a man] enter a second time into his mother's womb and be born?" Obviously, a literal understanding of Jesus' invitation to be born again is absurd; I imagine Nicodemus knows this even as he asks the question. What he doesn't know is what it might actually mean to be born again. I imagine that, like most of us, he's hoping for an answer that will help him feel better.

The Greek word that's usually translated "again" can also mean "anew" or "from the beginning" in something like the way musicians use the phrase "take it from the top." In that sense, Jesus' answer suggests that Nicodemus must start all over — reconsider everything he has thought he understood — lay aside his learning and authority, and the certainties of law and religion that have given structure to his life, and enter with an open heart and mind into a whole new relationship with God. It's a pretty scary proposition.

But the "being born" part isn't just a matter of "again." Being born "of the Spirit" is a brand new, first-time thing. I think we get so used to hearing the birth metaphor that it's easy for us to forget how radical it is. Some neuropsychologists say that birth is the most significant trauma people go through in the natural course of life. It's huge:

Birth is a transition from one state of life into another.

From living in water to living in air.

From total darkness to pervasive ambient light.

From total enclosure and protection to openness and vulnerability.

From isolation to community.

From a reliable, constant physical connection to the food source to a state in which you have to negotiate for what you need.

From total dependence to frightening separateness that is the beginning of a long adventure of relationship sought and shaped and developed in love.

It's very scary. At the most crucial learning moments in our lives, when we realize we have to change the habits of mind that have given us a sense of security, it can get very uncomfortable. I think of how often the disciples felt like that. When every expectation they had of how Jesus was going to go about being Israel's leader was disappointed, when the boat he slept on seemed to be sinking in the waves, when he was beaten and killed — the sense of safety may have been hard to hang on to. In order to stay in relationship with the One they loved and recognized as the Lord, they had to let go of every umbilical cord that tied them to community, family, and identity and take it from the top.

The birth metaphor is powerful. It is not a rejection of "the flesh," but a re-orientation: if we're attending to the spirit, matters of material life will fall into place. But we're called in this life to live the life the Spirit renews with every breath in the density of this flesh — fallen, fallible, hungry, and vulnerable — as Jesus did with us and for us.

Instead of an explanation, what Nicodemus gets is a bit of poetry and the biggest challenge he could possibly face — to invest in a kind of security that looks a lot like risk and trust in relationship with God — present and invisible — rather than rules.

Who do people say that I am?
MARK 8:27

Time and again Jesus leaves people scratching their heads and wondering, "Who is this man?" They are "amazed" and "murmur amongst themselves." The lame man who walked again, when asked who had healed him, didn't know. Jesus leaves a trail of people in his wake, profoundly disturbed and changed, scratching their heads and wondering who it is that has so unsettled them.

There are a lot of ways one might ask the question "Who is this man?" One might ask it in sheer puzzlement: "Who *is* this guy?" Or in fear and apprehension: "Who is this — some kind of troublemaker? What's he planning?" Or in jealousy and anger: "Who does he think he is?" Some of the people who encountered Jesus wanted to know who he was in order to follow him; others, in order to kill him.

Recognizing Jesus for who he was wasn't that simple then, and it's not that simple now. God chooses to whom he will reveal himself, and apparently, people don't recognize Jesus until some revelation comes to them. Those people scratching their heads and wondering who Jesus is don't get a straight answer. Sometimes Jesus just disappears from their midst. He makes himself clear to some and not to others. Why would he do that? If he came to die for all of us, and intended to send his message of hope to the whole world, why wouldn't he have come with a blast of trumpets, and a few headlines? Or at least a press release?

Evidently that's not God's way. God does reveal himself to us again and again, but not on our terms or our timing, and often in ways we tend to ignore: in Scripture, which many of us neglect to search with open hearts; in nature, which many of us ignore and even help destroy; in the faces of the poor and suffering, and of those it's given to us to love; in the events of ordinary life.

I have a friend who is in the habit of saying, when he's considering a baffling situation, "I wonder what God is up to here." He's cultivated the habit of expecting God to show himself precisely in odd, unsettling moments. He makes a practice of readiness for God to reveal himself. "I wonder what the Lord is up to here" means "I assume the Lord is present and at work — I just have to watch and wait, and I'll see him."

God works under pseudonyms. And when we wonder where he is, his answer to us is just the same as his answer to Andrew when he asked Jesus where he was staying so he could find and follow him: "Come and see." If we come, he'll help us see.

And Jacob was left alone. And a man *wrestled with him*
until the breaking of the day.

GENESIS 32:24

Wrestling is an intimate business. Two guys go to the mat and
try to pin each other down, working with tricky holds that the
good ones know the way chess players know their moves. They're
tough and wily and closely focused on each other. A good wrestler
knows his own and his opponent's strengths. There's even a kind
of trust involved — that both will obey the rules, that they're
not out to hurt or kill, but to test and prove their skills and to
win the point.

Jacob's match, of course, isn't a game; it's more like a birthing.
He's tired and bewildered and confused, but compelled to see
it through to the final blessing. A curious objective for such a
contest — a blessing.

Staying in relationship with God does sometimes involve
struggle — not just the struggle against temptation, but times
of prayer and discernment that are a lot like wrestling. Even reading the Bible can involve, in T. S. Eliot's words, an "intolerable
wrestle/with words and meanings" (from *East Coker*).

Language is messy. Words change over time, lose something in
translation, mean different things to different people, and become
contaminated by associations. Sometimes serious misunderstand-
ings happen because people are using the same words to mean

different things, or understand the words, but mistake the tone. The Bible is curious, strange, baffling, and, for most of us, culturally remote. It occurs to me to wonder what Bible those people read who sport the bumper sticker that says, "The Bible says it, I believe it, and that settles it." These people aren't wrestling; they're resting on their certainties. The Bible gives us what we need, alright, but it isn't a quick fix. It's an invitation to a relationship with an elusive, mysterious God who would apparently rather be misunderstood than be understood too simplistically.

In parables, apocalyptic symbols, and inconvenient silences, Scripture keeps inviting us: "Wrestle with this." It's hard to know what to do with the curses in the Psalms or some of Jesus' hard sayings, or his odd behavior — like withering a fig tree or sending a herd of swine over a cliff. It's hard to know why he knelt and wrote in the sand and left us no word about what he wrote. We like answers to our riddles. We like clarity, security, and certainty.

When I think about my most satisfying relationships, though, they all involve sometimes wrestling with unanticipated difficulties and differences. It is in that wrestling that we can arrive at more complex, mature, and adequate ways of understanding each other.

In the same way, when we wrestle with Scripture, we come into more intimate relationship with God. Sometimes we're hurt, like Jacob, in the process; sometimes we have to part company with people who don't want us to disagree with them. Sometimes we have to stay in a process that seems dubious, discouraging, or even a waste of time.

But we're not wasting our time; we're waiting for blessing. My favorite part of the Jacob story is his stubborn insistence on that blessing. Imagine if we read Scripture that way: I won't give up on this puzzling passage until I have received the blessing it offers. I may have to pray my way through it, come back to it tomorrow, ask a friend, or read a commentary to get another point of view, but there's a blessing here, and I want it.

The satisfactions of Scripture are not cheap. The Word is true, but not simple. If we want the blessing it offers, we have to cling to, and sometimes wrestle with, the God who embraces us with a strong and insistent hold even as we struggle, and will not let us go.

And he said to them, "*Suppose* one of you has a friend, and you go to him at midnight. . . ."

LUKE 11:5

This is how the story begins: "Suppose . . . ," or, as some translate the Greek, "Can you imagine. . . ." It's a beginning that invites listeners to participate with the heart and both sides of the brain in the situation the story unfolds — in this case about a man who, in fidelity to a strong community ethic of hospitality, gets up at an inconvenient hour and cares for an importunate friend.

"Suppose" invites us to hypothesize, to pretend, to feel our way into a story with empathy and compassion, because it could have been ours. We could have been the friend who needed food, or the friend who had to overcome irritation to get up and find some. We know we could have been on the spot in either of those ways because, if we've lived long enough, we have been on the spot in similar ways. We've been needy, and we've been in a position to provide for someone's needs, though possibly reluctant to do so at a bad time.

"Suppose" authorizes us to make of the story what we will, adapt it to the circumstances of our own lives and friendships, and explore it in light of our own possibly uncomfortable memories and tendencies. It makes us participants in the teaching moment, and gives us permission to arrive at our own "readings" of the situation before being asked to consider the conclusions Jesus offers — even those in the form of rhetorical questions that open doors of reflection rather than closing down on a dogma.

Jesus' teaching methods always direct us toward reflection rather than regulation, and toward compassion rather than commandment. Asking his listeners to "suppose" meets them in their imaginings, where intelligence is informed by the whole tangled cluster of experiences and losses and desires and resistances that individuals bring to the moment of learning.

I find in teaching that students sometimes don't take sufficient time to speculate — to play with possibilities on their way to the bottom line. Their intervals of "supposing" are reduced by the ready electronic availability of answers and expert opinion. But speculating, imagining, and supposing are an important part of the process by which we arrive at moral or spiritual insight. We need to "go there." We need to suppose that that friend in the night is our friend — a particular friend — and to see his or her face before us as we listen, so that the moral point, when we come to it, is something we have felt as well as figured out. Convictions not rooted deeply in feeling and imagination, and even in the life of the body, are planted in thin soil. Jesus knew this. So he invited those he loved to meet him in the intimate realm of imagination and do our learning there.

Works Cited

Ruth Angress. "A Colloquy with the Angel of Death." In *Kling-sor*, ed. Erika and Michael Metzger. Buffalo, N.Y.: SUNY, 1980.

W. H. Auden. "Leap Before You Look." *Collected Poems.* New York: Random House, 1976.

Wendell Berry. "IV." *A Timbered Choir.* Washington, D.C.: Counterpoint, 1998.

Annie Dillard. *Pilgrim at Tinker Creek.* In *Three by Annie Dillard.* New York: Harper Perennial, 1990.

Annie Dillard. *Teaching a Stone to Talk.* New York: Harper Perennial, 2000.

Gretel Ehrlich. *This Cold Heaven: Seven Seasons in Greenland.* New York: Pantheon, 2001.

T. S. Eliot. *East Coker.* In *Four Quartets,* in *T. S. Eliot: The Complete Poems and Plays, 1909-1950.* New York: Harcourt, Brace & World, 1971.

T. S. Eliot. *Little Gidding.* In *Four Quartets,* in *T. S. Eliot: The Complete Poems and Plays, 1909-1950.* New York: Harcourt, Brace & World, 1971.

Ralph Waldo Emerson. "The Rhodora." Reprinted at http://www.emersoncentral.com/poems/rhodora.htm.

Gerard Manley Hopkins. "Pied Beauty." In *Gerard Manley Hopkins: The Major Works.* Oxford: Oxford University Press, 2002.

Jeanne M. House. "Mystery of the Kabbalah: God as Energy." Find at http://www.reversespins.com/mysteryofthekabbalah.html.

Jane Kenyon. "Let Evening Come." In *Otherwise.* St. Paul, Minn.: Graywolf Press, 1996.

C. S. Lewis. *Perelandra.* New York: Macmillan, 1944.

William Bryant Logan. *Dirt: The Ecstatic Skin of the Earth.* New York: W. W. Norton, 2007.

Bill McKibben. *The Comforting Whirlwind: God, Job, and the Scale of Creation.* Cambridge, Mass.: Cowley Publications, 2005.

Naomi Shihab Nye. "Kindness." In *Words under the Words: Selected Poems.* Portland, Ore.: Eighth Mountain Press, 1994.

Robert Ochs, S.J. *God Is More Present than You Think.* Mahwah, N.J.: Paulist Press, 1970.

Mary Oliver. "Morning Poem." In *Selected Poems.* Boston: Beacon Press, 1992.

Mary Oliver. "The Plum Trees." In *American Primitive.* Boston: Back Bay Books, 1983.

Theodore Roethke. *The Waking.* New York: Anchor Books, 1975.

Marshall Rosenberg. *Nonviolent Communication: A Language of Life.* Encinitas, Calif.: Puddledancer Press, 2003.

Susan Sontag. "The Image-World." In *On Photography.* New York: Picador Press, 2001.

Works Cited

J. R. R. Tolkien. *The Fellowship of the Ring*. Boston: Houghton
 Mifflin, 1954, 1965.
Evelyn Waugh. *Brideshead Revisited*. Boston: Back Bay Books, 2012.
William Butler Yeats. "Lake Isle of Innisfree." In *The Collected
 Poems of W. B. Yeats*. New York: Macmillan, 1903, 1956.